SHAKESPEARE MADE EASY

Modern version side-by-side with full original text

Twelfth Night
or *What You Will*

Edited and rendered into modern English by
Alan Durband

Hutchinson

London   Melbourne   Sydney   Auckland   Johannesburg

Hutchinson & Co. (Publishers) Ltd
An imprint of the Hutchinson Publishing Group
17–21 Conway Street, London W1P 6JD

Hutchinson Publishing Group (Australia) Pty Ltd
PO Box 496, 16–22 Church Street, Hawthorne,
Melbourne, Victoria 3122

Hutchinson Group (NZ) Ltd
32–34 View Road, PO Box 40–086, Glenfield, Auckland 10

Hutchinson Group (SA) (Pty) Ltd
PO Box 337, Bergvlei 2012, South Africa

First published 1985
© Alan Durband 1985

Made Easy is a trade mark of Hutchinson Publishing Group Ltd

Set in Plantin and Univers by Colset Pte Ltd, Singapore

Printed in Great Britain by the Guernsey Press Co. Ltd., Guernsey,
Channel Islands

British Library Cataloguing in Publication Data
Shakespeare, William
    Twelfth Night
    I Title II Durband, Alan III Series
    822.3'3 PR 2837
ISBN 0 09 154781 4 (UK edition)
    0 09 940150 9 (export edition)

'*Reade him, therefore; and againe, and againe: And if then you do not like him, surely you are in some danger, not to understand him . . . .*'

John Hemming
Henry Condell

Preface to the 1623 Folio Edition

Shakespeare Made Easy

Titles in the series

Macbeth

Julius Caesar

The Merchant of Venice

Romeo and Juliet

Henry IV Part One

A Midsummer Night's Dream

Twelfth Night

Other drama books edited by Alan Durband

Contents

Introduction

Shakespeare Made Easy is intended for readers approaching the plays for the first time, who find the language of Elizabethan poetic drama an initial obstacle to understanding and enjoyment. In the past, the only answer to the problem has been to grapple with the difficulties with the aid of explanatory footnotes (often missing when they are most needed) and a stern teacher. Generations of students have complained that 'Shakespeare was ruined for me at school'.

Usually a fuller appreciation of Shakespeare's plays comes in later life, when the mind has matured and language skills are more developed. Often the desire to read Shakespeare for pleasure and enrichment follows from a visit to the theatre, where excellence of acting and production can bring to life qualities which sometimes lie dormant on the printed page.

Shakespeare Made Easy can never be a substitute for the original plays. It cannot possibly convey the full meaning of Shakespeare's poetic expression, which is untranslatable. *Shakespeare Made Easy* concentrates on the dramatic aspect, enabling the novice to become familiar with the plot and characters, and to experience one facet of Shakespeare's genius. To know and understand the central issues of each play is a sound starting point for further exploration and development.

Discretion can be used in choosing the best method to employ. One way is to read the original Shakespeare first, ignoring the modern translation or using it only when interest or understanding flags. Another way is to read the translation first, to establish confidence and familiarity with plots and characters.

Either way, cross-reference can be illuminating. The modern text can explain 'what is being said' if Shakespeare's language is particularly complex or his expression antiquated. The

Shakespeare text will show the reader of the modern paraphrase how much more can be expressed in poetry than in prose.

The use of *Shakespeare Made Easy* means that the newcomer need never be overcome by textual difficulties. From first to last, a measure of understanding is at hand – the key is provided for what has been a locked door to many students in the past. And as understanding grows, so an awareness develops of the potential of language as a vehicle for philosophic and moral expression, beauty, and the abidingly memorable.

Even professional Shakespearian scholars can never hope to arrive at a complete understanding of the plays. Each critic, researcher, actor or producer merely adds a little to the work that has already been done, or makes fresh interpretations of the texts for new generations. For everyone, Shakespearian appreciation is a journey. *Shakespeare Made Easy* is intended to help with the first steps.

William Shakespeare

His life

William Shakespeare was born in Stratford-on-Avon, Warwick-shire, on 23 April 1564, the son of a prosperous wool and lea-ther merchant. Very little is known of his early life. From parish records we know that he married Ann Hathaway in 1582, when he was eighteen, and she was twenty-six. They had three children, the eldest of whom died in childhood.

Between his marriage and the next thing we know about him, there is a gap of ten years. Probably he became a member of a travelling company of actors. By 1592 he had settled in London, and had earned a reputation as an actor and playwright.

Theatres were then in their infancy. The first (called *The Theatre*) was built by the actor James Burbage in 1576, in Shoreditch, then a suburb of London. Two more followed as the taste for theatre grew: *The Curtain* in 1577 and *The Rose* in 1587. The demand for new plays naturally increased. Shakespeare probably earned a living adapting old plays and working in collaboration with others on new ones. Today we would call him a 'freelance', since he was not permanently attached to one theatre.

In 1594, a new company of actors, The Lord Chamberlain's Men was formed, and Shakespeare was one of the shareholders. He remained a member throughout his working life. The Company was grouped in 1603, and re-named The King's Men, with James I as their patron.

Shakespeare and his fellow-actors prospered. In 1598 they built their own theatre, *The Globe*, which broke away from the traditional rectangular shape of the inn and its yard (the early home of travelling bands of actors). Shakespeare described it in *Henry V* as 'this wooden O', because it was circular.

Many other theatres were built by investors eager to profit from the new enthusiasm for drama. *The Hope*, *The Fortune*, *The Red Bull*, and *The Swan* were all open-air 'public' theatres. There were also many 'private' (or indoor) theatres, one of which (*The Blackfriars*) was purchased by Shakespeare and his friends because the child actors who performed there were dangerous competitors (Shakespeare denounces them in *Hamlet*).

After writing some thirty-seven plays (the exact number is something which scholars argue about), Shakespeare retired to his native Stratford, wealthy and respected. He died on his birthday, in 1616.

His plays

Shakespeare's plays were not all published in his lifetime. None of them comes to us exactly as he wrote it.

In Elizabethan times, plays were not regarded as either literature or good reading matter. They were written at speed (often by more than one writer), performed perhaps ten or twelve times, and then discarded. Fourteen of Shakespeare's plays were first printed in Quarto (17cm × 21cm) volumes, not all with his name as the author. Some were authorized (the 'good' Quartos) and probably were printed from prompt copies provided by the theatre. Others were pirated (the 'bad' Quartos) by booksellers who may have employed shorthand writers, or bought actors' copies after the run of the play had ended.

In 1623, seven years after Shakespeare's death, John Hemming and Henry Condell (fellow-actors and share-holders in The King's Men) published a collected edition of Shakespeare's works – thirty-six plays in all – in a Folio (21cm × 34cm) edition. From their introduction it would seem that they used Shakespeare's original manuscripts ('we have scarce received from him a blot in his papers') but the Folio volumes that still survive are not all exactly alike, nor are the plays printed as we know them today, with act and scene divisions and stage-directions.

A modern edition of a Shakespeare play is the result of a great deal of scholarly research and editorial skill over several centuries. The aim is always to publish a text (based on the good and bad Quartos and the Folio editions) that most closely resembles what Shakespeare intended. Misprints have added to the problems, so some words and lines are pure guesswork. This explains why some versions of Shakespeare's plays differ from others.

His theatre

The first purpose-built playhouse in Elizabethan London, constructed in 1576, was *The Theatre*. Its co-founders were John Brayne, an investor, and James Burbage, a carpenter turned actor. Like the six or seven 'public' (or outdoor) theatres which followed it over the next thirty years, it was situated outside the city, to avoid conflict with the authorities. They disapproved of players and playgoing, partly on moral and political grounds, and partly because of the danger of spreading the plague. (There were two major epidemics during Shakespeare's lifetime, and on each occasion the theatres were closed for lengthy periods.)

The Theatre was a financial success, and Shakespeare's company performed there until 1598, when a dispute over the lease of the land forced Burbage to take down the building. It was re-created in Southwark, as *The Globe*, with Shakespeare and several of his fellow-actors as the principal shareholders.

By modern standards, *The Globe* was small. Externally, the octagonal building measured less than thirty metres across, but in spite of this it could accommodate an audience of between two and three thousand people. (The largest of the three theatres at the National Theatre complex in London today seats 1160.)

Performances were advertised by means of playbills posted around the city, and they took place during the hours of day-

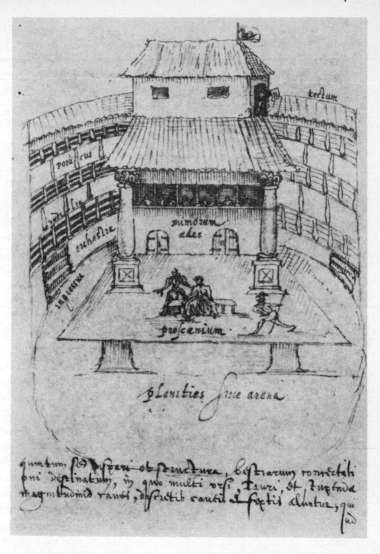

*Interior of the Swan Theatre – from a pen and ink drawing made
in 1596 (Mansell Collection)*

light when the weather was suitable. A flag flew to show that all was well, to save playgoers a wasted journey.

At the entrance, a doorkeeper collected one penny (about 60p in modern money) for admission to the 'pit' – a name taken from the old inn-yards, where bear-baiting and cock-fighting were popular sports. This was the minimum charge for seeing a play. The 'groundlings', as they were called, simply stood around the three sides of the stage, in the open air. Those who were better off could pay extra for a seat under cover. Stairs led from the pit to three tiers of galleries round the walls. The higher one went, the more one paid. The best seats cost one shilling, (or £6 today). In theatres owned by speculators like Francis Langley and Philip Henslowe, half the gallery takings went to the landlord.

A full house might consist of 800 groundlings and 1500 in the galleries, with a dozen more exclusive seats on the stage itself for the gentry. A new play might run for between six and sixteen performances; the average was about ten. As there were no breaks between scenes, and no intervals, most plays could be performed in two hours. A trumpet sounded three times before the play began.

The acting company assembled in the Tiring House at the rear of the stage. This was where they 'attired' (or dressed) themselves: not in costumes representing the period of the play, but in Elizabethan doublet and hose. All performances were therefore in modern dress, though no expense was spared to make the stage costumes lavish. The entire company was male. By law actresses were not allowed, and female roles were performed by boys.

Access to the stage from the Tiring House was through two doors, one on each side of the stage. Because there was no front curtain, every entrance had to have its corresponding exit, so an actor killed on stage had to be carried off. There was no scenery: the audience used its imagination, guided by the spoken word. Storms and night scenes might well be performed on sunny days in mid-afternoon; the Elizabethan playgoer relied entirely on the playwrights' descriptive skills to establish the dramatic atmosphere.

Once on stage, the actors and their expensive clothes were protected from sudden showers by a canopy, the underside of which was painted blue, and spangled with stars to represent the heavens. A trapdoor in the stage made ghostly entrances and the gravedigging scene in *Hamlet* possible. Behind the main stage, in between the two entrance doors, there was a curtained area, concealing a small inner stage, useful for bedroom scenes. Above this was a balcony, which served for castle walls (as in *Henry V*) or a domestic balcony (as in the famous scene in *Romeo and Juliet*).

The acting style in Elizabethan times was probably more declamatory than we favour today, but the close proximity of the audience also made a degree of intimacy possible. In those days soliloquies and asides seemed quite natural. Act and scene divisions did not exist (those in printed versions of the play today have been added by editors), but Shakespeare often indicates a scene-ending by a rhyming couplet.

A company such as The King's Men at *The Globe* would consist of around twenty-five actors, half of whom might be shareholders, and the rest part-timers engaged for a particular play. Amongst the shareholders in *The Globe* were several specialists – William Kempe, for example, was a renowned comedian and Robert Armin was a singer and dancer. Playwrights wrote parts to suit the actors who were available, and devised ways of overcoming the absence of women. Shakespeare often has his heroines dress as young men, and physical contact between lovers was formal compared with the realism we expect today.

His verse

Shakespeare wrote his plays mostly in blank verse: that is,

unrhymed lines consisting of ten syllables, alternately stressed and unstressed. The technical term for this form is the 'iambic pentameter'. When Shakespeare first began to write for the stage, it was fashionable to maintain this regular beat from the first line of the play till the last.

Shakespeare conformed at first, and then experimented. Some of his early plays contain whole scenes in rhyming couplets – in *Romeo and Juliet*, for example, there is extensive use of rhyme, and as if to show his versatility, Shakespeare even inserts a sonnet into the dialogue.

But as he matured, he sought greater freedom of expression than rhyme allowed. Rhyme is still used to indicate a scene-ending, or to stress lines which he wishes the audience to remember. Generally, though, Shakespeare moved towards the rhythms of everyday speech. This gave him many dramatic advantages, which he fully and subtly exploits in terms of atmosphere, character, emotion, stress and pace.

It is Shakespeare's poetic imagery, however, that most distinguishes his verse from that of lesser playwrights. It enables him to stretch the imagination, express complex thought-patterns in memorable language, and convey a number of associated ideas in a compressed and economical form. A study of Shakespeare's imagery – especially in his later plays – is often the key to a full understanding of his meaning and purposes.

At the other extreme is prose. Shakespeare normally reserves it for servants, clowns, commoners, and pedestrian matters such as lists, messages and letters.

Twelfth Night or *What You Will*

Date

Francis Meres, in his *Wit's Treasury*, lists all the plays Shakespeare had written up to 1598, and *Twelfth Night* is not mentioned. The first known reference to it is in John Manningham's diary entry of 2 February 1602. Scholars believe the play was first performed in 1601, at an entertainment before Queen Elizabeth, who was then host to an Italian nobleman, Don Virginio Orsino: the date was 6 January, the twelfth night after Christmas, and this would account for the otherwise irrelevant main title.

Source

Stories and plays involving mistaken identity, disguise, and unrequited love were very common in the sixteenth century and no direct source has been traced for the plot of *Twelfth Night*. A play called *The Deceived* (1592), or a story in a collection written by Barnaby Riche (1581) may have given Shakespeare the basic idea for his main plot, but other than providing him with a stock situation and starting-point, the links are only of very minor significance.

Text

Twelfth Night was first published in the Folio Edition of 1623. The editors appear to have used an uncomplicated manuscript, which all subsequent editions have followed with only small textual amendments.

Twelfth Night

Original text and modern version

The characters

Orsino   Duke of Illyria
Sebastian   Viola's brother
Antonio   a Sea Captain, Sebastian's friend
Valentine }
Curio }   gentlemen attending on the Duke
Sir Toby Belch   Olivia's uncle
Sir Andrew Aguecheek
Malvolio   Olivia's steward
Fabian }
Feste the Clown }   Olivia's servants
A Sea Captain   Viola's friend
Olivia   a rich Countess
Viola   in love with Orsino
Maria   Olivia's woman
Lords, Priests, Sailors, Officers, Musicians and other
Attendants

Act one

Scene 1

The Duke's Palace. Enter **Duke, Curio, Lords, Musicians** *attending*

Duke If music be the food of love, play on;
 Give me excess of it, that, surfeiting,
 The appetite may sicken, and so die.
 That strain again! It had a dying fall;
5 O, it came o'er my ear like the sweet sound
 That breathes upon a bank of violets,
 Stealing and giving odour. Enough! no more;
 'Tis not so sweet now as it was before.
 O spirit of love! how quick and fresh art thou,
10 That, notwithstanding thy capacity
 Receiveth as the sea, nought enters there,
 Of what validity and pitch soe'er,
 But falls into abatement and low price,
 Even in a minute; so full of shapes is fancy
15 That it alone is high fantastical.

Curio Will you go hunt, my lord?

Duke   What, Curio?

Curio   The hart.

Duke Why, so I do, the noblest that I have.
 O, when mine eyes did see Olivia first,
20 Methought she purged the air of pestilence;
 That instant was I turned into a hart,
 And my desires, like fell and cruel hounds,
 E'er since pursue me.

Act one

Scene 1

Duke Orsino's palace in Illyria. The **Duke** *enters, followed by* **Curio** [*an equerry*], *and* **Lords. Musicians** *are playing softly in the background. The music is about to end, but the* **Duke,** *who is in a love-sick mood, gestures for them to continue.*

Duke If music is love's food, play on. Give me too much of it: by gorging, the appetite may sicken and so die. That chord again! It had a melancholy tone. To my ear it was like the sweet sound of a breeze that gently blows upon a bank of violets, stealing the perfumes and bringing others of its own. [*He listens briefly, but is impatient*] That's enough. Stop there: it's not so pleasing now as it was before. [*He sighs*] O, spirit of love! How lively and insatiable you are! In spite of having a capacity like that of the sea, nothing comes to you, no matter how precious or excellent it may be, without immediately becoming diminished and worthless. Love has such variety that nothing can keep up with its demands.

Curio Would you like to go hunting, my lord?

Duke Hunt what, Curio?

Curio The hart.

Duke That's what I'm doing. [*He places his hand on his heart*] It's the dearest part of me. When I first saw Olivia, I thought she purified the air. That very instant I became a hart, and my desires – like fierce and cruel hounds – have pursued me ever since.

21

Enter **Valentine**

How now! What news from her?

Valentine   So please my lord, I might not be admitted;
25   But from her handmaid do return this answer;
The element itself, till seven years' heat,
Shall not behold her face at ample view;
But, like a cloistress, she will veiled walk,
And water once a day her chamber round
30   With eye-offending brine; all this to season
A brother's dead love, which she would keep fresh
And lasting in her sad remembrance.

Duke   O, she that hath a heart of that fine frame
To pay this debt of love but to a brother,
35   How will she love, when the rich golden shaft
Hath killed the flock of all affections else
That live in her; when liver, brain, and heart,
These sovereign thrones, are all supplied, and filled
Her sweet perfections, with one self king!
40   Away before me to sweet beds of flowers;
Love-thoughts lie rich when canopied with bowers.

[*Exeunt*]

Scene 2

The sea-coast. Enter **Viola, a Captain** *and* **Sailors**

Viola   What country, friends, is this?

Captain   This is Illyria, lady.

[**Valentine**, *another equerry, enters*]

Well? What news from her?

Valentine   My lord, I wasn't invited in. Through her
maidservant, the answer is this: she will not show her face
in public for seven years. Instead, she will wear the veil like
a nun, weeping salt tears once a day around her room; all
this to commemorate her love for her dead brother, which
she wishes to preserve in her sad memory.

Duke   The woman who has the tenderness of heart to make
this sacrifice for a mere brother, why, how will she love
when Cupid's dart has killed all other claims to her affection
dwelling within her; when her emotions, her judgement and
her love – those normally independent qualities – are all
ruled by one single passion, which supplies all her needs and
fulfils all her sweet perfections! Lead the way to the flower
garden. Love thoughts are best indulged in natural
surroundings. . . .

[*They go*]

Scene 2

The sea-coast of Illyria. Enter **Viola**, *a* **Sea-captain**, *and* **Sailors**.
They have just survived a shipwreck

Viola   What's this country, friends?

Captain   This is Illyria, my lady.

Viola   And what should I do in Illyria?
My brother he is in Elysium:
Perchance he is not drowned; what think you, sailors?

5 **Captain**   It is perchance that you yourself were saved.

Viola   O, my poor brother! And so perchance may he be.

Captain   True, madam; and, to comfort you with chance,
Assure yourself, after our ship did split,
When you and those poor number saved with you
10   Hung on our driving boat, I saw your brother,
Most provident in peril, bind himself,
Courage and hope both teaching him the practice,
To a strong mast that lived upon the sea;
Where, like Arion on the dolphin's back,
15   I saw him hold acquaintance with the waves
So long as I could see.

Viola   For saying so, there's gold;
Mine own escape unfoldeth to my hope,
Whereto thy speech serves for authority,
20   The like of him. Know'st thou this country?

Captain   Ay, madam, well; for I was bred and born
Not three hours' travel from this very place.

Viola   Who governs here?

Captain   A noble duke, in nature as in name.

25 **Viola**   What is his name?

Captain   Orsino.

Viola   Orsino! I have heard my father name him;
He was a bachelor then.

Captain   And so is now, or was so very late;
30   For but a month ago I went from hence,
And then 'twas fresh in murmur – as, you know,

Viola   What am I doing in Illyria? My brother's in heaven! With
luck he hasn't drowned. What do you think, sailors?

Captain   It's with luck that you yourself were saved.

Viola   Oh, my poor brother! Perhaps he may be, too.

Captain   True madam, and to comfort you with possibilities,
be assured that after our ship split, when you and the few
who were saved with you clung to our drifting vessel, I saw
your brother – wisely in the perilous circumstances – tie
himself to a stout mast that was floating in the sea, courage
and hope teaching him what best to do. There, like Arion in
the Greek myth, who escaped from murder on the back of a
dolphin, I saw him ride the waves as long as I could keep
him in sight.

Viola   [*giving him money*] For saying that, here's gold. The
fact that I escaped gives me hope that he will do so too, and
your words back this up. Do you know this country?

Captain   Yes, madam, well. I was born and bred not three
hours' journey from here.

Viola   Who rules the place?

Captain   A noble duke, both by birth and inclination.

Viola   What's his name?

Captain   Orsino.

Viola   Orsino! I've heard my father mention him. He was a
bachelor then.

Captain   And still is, or was till recently. I left here a month
ago, and then it was freshly rumoured – as you know,

> What great ones do the less will prattle of –
> That he did seek the love of fair Olivia.

Viola   What's she?

35 **Captain**   A virtuous maid, the daughter of a count
> That died some twelvemonth since, then leaving her
> In the protection of his son, her brother,
> Who shortly also died; for whose dear love,
> They say, she hath abjured the company
> And sight of men.

40 **Viola**   O that I served that lady,
> And might not be delivered to the world
> Till I had made mine own occasion mellow,
> What my estate is!

Captain   That were hard to compass,
> Because she will admit no kind of suit,
45 No, not the duke's.

Viola   There is a fair behaviour in thee, captain;
> And though that nature with a beauteous wall
> Doth oft close in pollution, yet of thee
> I will believe thou hast a mind that suits
50 With this thy fair and outward character.
> I prithee, and I'll pay thee bounteously,
> Conceal me what I am, and be my aid
> For such disguise as haply shall become
> The form of my intent. I'll serve this duke;
55 Thou shalt present me as an eunuch to him;
> It may be worth thy pains; for I can sing
> And speak to him in many sorts of music
> That will allow me very worth his service.
> What else may hap, to time I will commit;
60 Only shape thou thy silence to my wit.

Captain   Be you his eunuch, and your mute I'll be;

ordinary folk will chatter about nobility – that he was hoping to win the fair Olivia.

Viola   Who's she?

Captain   A virtuous young lady, the daughter of a Count who died about twelve months ago. He left her under the protection of his son, her brother, who shortly afterwards also died. For his dear love, they say, she has renounced the company and sight of men.

Viola   Would that I could serve that lady, and that I could avoid publicity till I know better what my situation is!

Captain   That would not be easy, because she won't consider any pleas, not even the Duke's.

Viola   You seem a decent man, captain, and though nature frequently encloses foul things in a beautiful wrapper, in your case I'll believe your mind matches your civil appearance. Will you therefore – I'll pay you handsomely – conceal who I am, and help me in whatever disguise best suits my purposes? I'll serve this Duke. You must introduce me to him as a eunuch. It'll be worth your trouble, because I can sing and speak to him in various musical ways, which will make me an attractive employee. What follows, time will tell. Just keep mum, as I think fit.

Captain   If you'll be his eunuch, I'll be your dumb servant. If

When my tongue blabs, then let mine eyes not see.

Viola   I thank thee; lead me on.

[*Exeunt*]

Scene 3

Olivia's house. Enter **Sir Toby Belch** *and* **Maria**

Sir Toby   What a plague means my niece, to take the death of her brother thus? I am sure care's an enemy to life.

Maria   By my troth, Sir Toby, you must come in earlier o' nights; your cousin, my lady, takes great exceptions to your
5   ill hours.

Sir Toby   Why, let her except before excepted.

Maria   Ay, but you must confine yourself within the modest limits of order.

Sir Toby   Confine? I'll confine myself no finer than I am.
10   These clothes are good enough to drink in, and so be these boots too; an they be not, let them hang themselves in their own straps.

Maria   That quaffing and drinking will undo you; I heard my lady talk of it yesterday; and of a foolish knight that you
15   brought in one night here to be her wooer.

Sir Toby   Who? Sir Andrew Aguecheek?

my tongue ever blabs, may I go blind!

Viola   Thank you. [*She gestures*] After you . . .

[*They leave*]

Scene 3

A room in the house of Olivia. Enter **Sir Toby Belch**, *a large, fat man, and* **Maria**, Olivia's maid

Sir Toby   What the devil does my niece mean by taking her brother's death like this? I'm sure worrying isn't good for one's health.

Maria   Really, Sir Toby, you must come home earlier at night. Your cousin, my lady, takes great exception to your irregular hours.

Sir Toby   She's welcome to her exceptions so long as I'm one of them.

Maria   Yes, but you must confine yourself to what's reasonable and proper.

Sir Toby   Confine? I'll confine myself to finery no finer than I'm in. These clothes are good enough to drink in, and so are these boots, too. If they're not, they can hang themselves in their own laces.

Maria   This tippling and drinking will be the ruin of you. I heard my mistress talk about it yesterday, and about a foolish knight that you brought home one night to be her wooer.

Sir Toby   Who? Sir Andrew Aguecheek?

Maria   Ay, he.

Sir Toby   He's as tall a man as any's in Illyria.

Maria   What's that to the purpose?

20 **Sir Toby**   Why, he has three thousand ducats a year.

Maria   Ay, but he'll have but a year in all these ducats; he's a very fool and a prodigal.

Sir Toby   Fie, that you'll say so! He plays o' the viol-de-gamboys, and speaks three or four languages word for word
25   without book, and hath all the good gifts of nature.

Maria   He hath indeed, almost natural; for besides that he's a fool, he's a great quarreller; and but that he hath the gift of a coward to allay the gust he hath in quarrelling, 'tis thought among the prudent he would quickly have the gift of a grave.

30 **Sir Toby**   By this hand, they are scoundrels and substractors that say so of him. Who are they?

Maria   They that add, moreover, he's drunk nightly in your company.

Sir Toby   With drinking healths to my niece. I'll drink to her
35   as long as there is a passage in my throat and drink in Illyria. He's a coward and a coystril that will not drink to my niece till his brains turn o' the toe like a parish-top. What, wench! Castiliano vulgo! for here comes Sir Andrew Agueface.

[*Enter* **Sir Andrew Aguecheek**]

Sir Andrew   Sir Toby Belch! How now, Sir Toby Belch!

40 **Sir Toby**   Sweet Sir Andrew!

Maria   Yes, him.

Sir Toby   He's the equal of any man in Illyria.

Maria   In what way?

Sir Toby   Why, his income is three thousand ducats a year.

Maria   Yes, but he'll have spent all his ducats in the first twelve months. He's a real fool and a spendthrift.

Sir Toby   Shame on you for saying so! He can play the violin; he speaks three or four languages word for word off by heart; and he's got all nature's finest gifts.

Maria   He has indeed, like a born idiot. Besides being a fool, he's a great quarreller, and if he hadn't also got the gift of cowardice to moderate the enthusiasm he has for quarrelling, it's generally thought by those with brains that he'd quickly have the gift of a grave!

Sir Toby   By this hand [*he raises one*] they are scoundrels and [*'detractors' is the word he wants but he's too fuddled to find it*] subtractors who say that about him. Who are they?

Maria   Those who, in addition [*she can't resist the easy joke*], say he's drunk every night in your company.

Sir Toby   [*all injured innocence*] With drinking my niece's health! I'll drink to her as long as there's a passage in my throat and drink in Illyria. He's a coward and a cad who won't drink to my niece till his brains reel like a spinning top. What, wench? Speak of the devil – here comes Sir Andrew Agueface!

[**Sir Andrew Aguecheek** *enters. He is as lanky as* **Sir Toby** *is fat*]

Sir Andrew   Sir Toby Belch! Greetings, Sir Toby Belch!

Sir Toby   [*embracing him*] Sweet Sir Andrew!

Sir Andrew   Bless you, fair shrew.

Maria   And you too, sir.

Sir Toby   Accost, Sir Andrew, accost.

Sir Andrew   What's that?

45 **Sir Toby**   My niece's chambermaid.

Sir Andrew   Good Mistress Accost, I desire better
acquaintance.

Maria   My name is Mary, sir.

Sir Andrew   Good Mistress Mary Accost –

50 **Sir Toby**   You mistake, knight; 'accost' is front her, board her,
woo her, assail her.

Sir Andrew   By my troth, I would not undertake her in this
company. Is that the meaning of 'accost'?

Maria   Fare you well, gentlemen.

55 **Sir Toby**   An thou let part so, Sir Andrew, would thou
might'st never draw sword again!

Sir Andrew   An you part so, mistress, I would I might never
draw sword again. Fair lady, do you think you have fools in
hand?

60 **Maria**   Sir, I have not you by the hand.

Sir Andrew   Marry, but you shall have; and here's my hand.

Maria   Now, sir, 'thought is free'; I pray you, bring your hand
to the buttery-bar and let it drink.

Sir Andrew   [*to* **Maria**] Bless you, dear shrew. [*He thinks it's a compliment*]

Maria   [*curtseying, keeping a straight face*] And you too, sir.

Sir Toby   [*nudging him*] Accost her, Sir Andrew; accost her.

Sir Andrew   [*baffled by a new word*] What does that mean?

Sir Toby   [*winking and nudging meaningfully*] My niece's chambermaid . . .

Sir Andrew   [*misunderstanding*] Dear Miss Accost. I'd like to know you better

Maria   [*demurely*] My name is Mary, sir.

Sir Andrew   Dear Miss *Mary* Accost –

Sir Toby   [*interrupting*] You've got it wrong, knight. 'Accost' means make advances to her; take her on; flirt with her; go into the attack.

Sir Andrew   My word, I wouldn't tackle her in this company. Is that what 'accost' means?

Maria   [*turning to go*] Goodbye, gentlemen!

Sir Toby   If you let her go like that, Sir Andrew, may you never draw your sword again!

Sir Andrew   If you go like that, madam, I hope I never draw my sword again. Dear lady, do you think you are handling fools?

Maria   Sir, I'm not handling you.

Sir Andrew   Well, you will. Here's my hand. [*He offers it to her*]

Maria   There's no charge for hoping. Have this for free. [*She takes hold of it*]

33

Sir Andrew   Wherefore, sweetheart? What's your metaphor?

65 **Maria**   It's dry, sir.

Sir Andrew   Why, I think so; I am not such an ass but I can keep my hand dry. But what's your jest?

Maria   A dry jest, sir.

Sir Andrew   Are you full of them?

70 **Maria**   Ay, sir, I have them at my fingers' ends; marry, now I let go your hand, I am barren.

[*Exit*]

Sir Toby   O knight! thou lackest a cup of canary; when did I see thee so put down?

Sir Andrew   Never in your life, I think; unless you see canary 75 put me down. Methinks sometimes I have no more wit than a Christian or an ordinary man has; but I am a great eater of beef, and I believe that does harm to my wit.

Sir Toby   No question.

Sir Andrew   An I thought that, I'd forswear it. I'll ride home 80 tomorrow, Sir Toby.

Sir Toby   Pourquoi, my dear knight?

Sir Andrew   What is 'pourquoi'? Do or not do? I would I had bestowed that time in the tongues that I have in fencing, dancing, and bear-baiting. Oh, had I but followed the arts!

85 **Sir Toby**   Then hadst thou had an excellent head of hair.

Sir Andrew   How do you mean, sweetheart? What are you hinting at?

Maria   [*looking at his palm; a clammy one indicates passion*] It's dry, sir.

Sir Andrew   I should hope so. I'm not so silly that I can't keep my hand dry. But what's your little joke?

Maria   A silly one, sir.

Sir Andrew   Are you full of them?

Maria   Yes, sir; they're at my finger's ends. [*She extends hers till they cease to make contact with* **Sir Andrew's**] Now I let your hand go, I've no more left . . .

[*She leaves, victorious*]

Sir Toby   Oh, knight! You need a glass of wine. Whenever have I seen you so put down!

Sir Andrew   Never in all your life, I think, unless you've seen wine put me down! Sometimes I think I've no more brains than a Christian has, or an ordinary sort of man. But I eat a lot of beef, and I think that does some harm to my wits.

Sir Toby   No doubt about it.

Sir Andrew   If I really thought that, I'd give it up. [*Pause*] I'll ride back home tomorrow, Sir Toby.

Sir Toby   [*using the French for 'why'*] Pourquoi, my dear knight?

Sir Andrew   [*puzzled*] What does 'pourquoi' mean? Go or not go? I wish I'd devoted as much time to languages as I have to fencing, dancing and bear-baiting. Oh, if only I'd pursued the Arts!

Sir Toby   Then you'd have had a fine head of hair.

35

Sir Andrew   Why, would that have mended my hair?

Sir Toby   Past question; for thou seest it will not curl by nature.

Sir Andrew   But it becomes me well enough, does it not?

90 **Sir Toby**   Excellent; it hangs like flax on a distaff, and I hope to see a housewife take thee between her legs, and spin it off.

Sir Andrew   Faith, I'll home tomorrow, Sir Toby; your niece will not be seen; or if she be, it's four to one she'll none of me. The count himself here hard by woos her.

95 **Sir Toby**   She'll none o' the count; she'll not match above her degree, neither in estate, years, nor wit; I have heard her swear it. Tut, there's life in't, man.

Sir Andrew   I'll stay a month longer. I am a fellow o' the strangest mind i' the world; I delight in masques and revels
100   sometimes altogether.

Sir Toby   Art thou good at these kickshawses, knight?

Sir Andrew   As any man in Illyria, whatsoever he be, under the degree of my betters; and yet I will not compare with an old man.

105 **Sir Toby**   What is thy excellence in a galliard, knight?

Sir Andrew   Faith, I can cut a caper.

Sir Toby   And I can cut the mutton to 't.

Sir Andrew   And I think I have the back-trick simply as strong as any man in Illyria.

Sir Andrew   [*feeling his lanky locks*] Why, would Arts improve my hair?

Sir Toby   Beyond all doubt. You can see it doesn't curl naturally.

Sir Andrew   But it suits me, doesn't it?

Sir Toby   Excellently. It hangs like wool from a spindle. I hope to see a housewife take you between her legs, have it off you, and spin it.

Sir Andrew   Truly, I'll go home tomorrow, Sir Toby. I can't get to see your niece, and if I did, it's four to one she'd have nothing to do with me. The Count himself who lives near here is wooing her.

Sir Toby   She'll have no truck with the Count. She won't marry above herself, either in fortune, age, or intelligence. I've heard her swear it. Nonsense: you stand a good chance, man!

Sir Andrew   I'll stay one more month. I'm a fellow with a quirky kind of mind: I love masques and revels, sometimes both together.

Sir Toby   Are you good at such trivia, knight?

Sir Andrew   [*proudly*] As any man in Illyria, whoever he may be, provided he's my inferior. But I'm not as good as an experienced man.

Sir Toby   How good are you at a reel, knight?

Sir Andrew   'Strewth, I can cut a caper! [*He means the dance, not the pickle bearing the same name*]

Sir Toby   And I can cut the mutton to go with it! [*He means the pickle, not the dance*]

Sir Andrew   I think I can do the back-step as neatly as any man in Illyria. [*He demonstrates feebly*]

37

110 **Sir Toby**   Wherefore are these things hid? Wherefore have
these gifts a curtain before 'em? Are they like to take dust,
like Mistress Mall's picture? Why dost thou not go to church
in a galliard, and come home in a coranto? My very walk
should be a jig; I would not so much as make water but in a
115 sink-a-pace. What dost thou mean? Is it a world to hide virtues in? I did think, by the excellent constitution of thy leg,
it was formed under the star of a galliard.

   Sir Andrew   Ay, 'tis strong, and it does indifferent well in a
flame-coloured stock. Shall we set about some revels?

120 **Sir Toby**   What shall we do else? Were we not born under
Taurus?

   Sir Andrew   Taurus! that's sides and heart.

   Sir Toby   No, sir, it is legs and thighs. Let me see thee caper.
Ha! higher; ha, ha! excellent!

                                           [*Exeunt*]

Scene 4

The Duke's Palace. Enter **Valentine,** *and* **Viola** *in man's attire*

   Valentine   If the duke continue these favours towards you,
Cesario, you are like to be much advanced: he hath known
you but three days and already you are no stranger.

Sir Toby   [*in mock admiration*] Why are these things kept
secret? Why have these talents been hidden behind a
curtain? Are they likely to get dusty, like the Mona Lisa?
Why don't you reel your way to Church, and come home
doing a fling? If I were you, my very *walk* would be a jig: I
wouldn't so much as pass water unless it was to a lively
rhythm. I ask you: is it the kind of world to hide virtues in?
Looking at the excellent shape of your leg, I thought it must
have been formed under the influence of a dancing star!

Sir Andrew   [*naively*] Yes, it's strong: and it looks rather good
in a flame-coloured stocking. Shall we do some revelling?

Sir Toby   What shall we do else? Were we not born under the
sign of Taurus?

Sir Andrew   Taurus? That influences sides and the heart . . .

Sir Toby   No, sir – legs and thighs! [*In fact it was necks and
throats, but* **Sir Andrew** *wouldn't know any better*] Let me
see you dance. [**Sir Andrew** *obliges again*] Higher! [**Sir
Andrew** *does his feeble best*] Ha, ha! Excellent!

[*They go off together*]

Scene 4

A room in the Duke's place. Enter **Valentine** *and* **Viola**, *who is
dressed as a young man, and now is known as* **Cesario**

Valentine   If the Duke continues to favour you, Cesario, you're
likely to be promoted. He's known you only three days, and
already you are well in.

Viola   You either fear his humour or my negligence, that you
5   call in question the continuance of his love. Is he inconstant,
sir, in his favours?

Valentine   No, believe me.

Viola   I thank you. Here comes the count.

[*Enter* **Duke, Curio** *and* **Attendants**]

Duke   Who saw Cesario, ho?

10 **Viola**   On your attendance, my lord; here.

Duke   Stand you awhile aloof. Cesario,
Thou know'st no less but all; I have unclasped
To thee the book even of my secret soul.
Therefore, good youth, address thy gait unto her;
15   Be not denied access, stand at her doors,
And tell them, there thy fixed foot shall grow
Till thou have audience.

Viola   Sure, my noble lord,
If she be so abandoned to her sorrow
As it is spoke, she never will admit me.

20 **Duke**   Be clamorous, and leap all civil bounds,
Rather than make unprofited return.

Viola   Say I do speak with her, my lord; what then?

Duke   O! then unfold the passion of my love;
Surprise her with discourse of my dear faith;
25   It shall become thee well to act my woes;
She will attend it better in thy youth
Than in a nuncio's of more grave aspect.

Viola   I think not so, my lord.

Duke   Dear lad, believe it;
For they shall yet belie thy happy years

40

Viola   In doubting that his love will continue, either you fear his moods or think I'll become neglectful. Is he fickle, sir, in bestowing his favours?

Valentine   No, believe me.

Viola   I thank you. Here comes the Count.

[*The* **Duke** *enters, with* **Curio** *and* **Attendants**]

Duke   Has anyone seen Cesario?

Viola   Here at your service, my lord.

Duke   [*to his* **Attendants**] Stand aside for a moment. [*To* **Viola**] Cesario, you know everything: all the innermost secrets of my soul are an open book to you. Therefore, young man, go to her. Don't be denied access. Stand outside her doors, and tell them your foot will take root till you're granted an audience.

Viola   Surely, my noble lord, if she's so committed to her mourning as people say, she'll never let me in?

Duke   Make a fuss and disregard good manners rather than come back unsuccessful.

Viola   Supposing I do speak to her, my lord, what then?

Duke   Oh, then you must reveal my passionate love, and surprise her with talk of my sincere devotion. It'll be appropriate for *you* to convey my distress – she'll take more notice of it coming from a youth rather than an older messenger.

Viola   I don't think so, my lord.

Duke   Dear boy, take my word for it. They'd be denying you the happy days of adolescence if they described you as a

30   That say thou art a man; Diana's lip
      Is not more smooth and rubious; thy small pipe
      Is as the maiden's organ, shrill and sound,
      And all is semblative a woman's part.
      I know thy constellation is right apt
35   For this affair. Some four or five attend him;
      All, if you will; for I myself am best
      When least in company. Prosper well in this,
      And thou shalt live as freely as thy lord,
      To call his fortune thine.

Viola   I'll do my best
40   Too woo your lady. (*Aside*) Yet, a barful strife!
      Whoe'er I woo, myself would be his wife.

                                          [*Exeunt*]

Scene 5

Olivia's House. Enter **Maria** *and* **Feste,** *the clown*

Maria   Nay, either tell me where thou hast been, or I will not
open my lips so wide as a bristle may enter in way of thy
excuse. My lady will hang thee for thy absence.

Feste   Let her hang me; he that is well hanged in this world
5   needs to fear no colours.

Maria   Make that good.

Feste   He shall see none to fear.

Maria   A good lenten answer; I can tell thee where that saying
was born, of 'I fear no colours'.

man. The goddess Diana's lip is not so smooth and red as
yours. Your high voice is like a maiden's, shrill and firm; and
overall you'd pass for a woman. I know your character is
just right for this business. [*To the* **Attendants**] Four or five
of you go with him. All of you, if you wish, because I'm
better left on my own. Succeed in this, and you'll live as
well as your lord, sharing his good fortune.

Viola   I'll do my best to woo your lady. [*Aside, to herself*] A
difficult task! Though I may woo others, I'd like to be his
wife myself.

[*They go*]

Scene 5

A room in Olivia's house. Enter **Maria** *and* **Feste**, the clown

Maria   No: either tell me where you have been, or I won't open
my mouth to make excuses for you by so much as the width
of a bristle! My lady will hang you for going missing.

Feste   Let her hang me. A man who is well hanged in this
world has no need to 'fear the colours'.

Maria   How do you make that out?

Feste   He won't be able to see any to fear!

Maria   That's a good straightforward answer. I can tell you
where that expression 'I fear no colours' comes from.

10 **Feste**   Where, good Mistress Mary?

Maria   In the wars; and that may you be bold to say in your
foolery.

Feste   Well, God give them wisdom that have it; and those
that are fools, let them use their talents.

15 **Maria**   Yet you will be hanged for being so long absent; or, to
be turned away, is not that as good as a hanging to you?

Feste   Many a good hanging prevents a bad marriage; and, for
turning away, let summer bear it out.

Maria   You are resolute, then?

20 **Feste**   Not so, neither; but I am resolved on two points.

Maria   That if one break, the other will hold; or, if both
break, your gaskins fall.

Feste   Apt, in good faith; very apt. Well, go thy way; if Sir
Toby would leave drinking, thou wert as witty a piece of
25 Eve's flesh as any in Illyria.

Maria   Peace, you rogue, no more o' that. Here comes my
lady; make your excuse wisely, you were best.

[*Exit*]

Feste   Wit, an 't be thy will, put me into good fooling! Those
wits that think they have thee, do very oft prove fools; and I,
30 that am sure I lack thee, may pass for a wise man; for what
says Quinapalus? 'Better a witty fool than a foolish wit.'

Feste   Where, Miss Mary?

Maria   From warfare. [*Armies always displayed their 'colours',
or flags, in battle*] Now you can use it with confidence in
your foolish patter.

Feste   Well, may God give wisdom to the wise. As to the
fools – they must use their brains.

Maria   Still, you'll be hanged for being absent so long. Or
you'll be sacked. Wouldn't that be as bad as hanging to
you?

Feste   Many a good hanging prevents a bad marriage. As for
being sacked, at least it's summer.

Maria   You are adamant, then?

Feste   No, not really. But I've braced myself on two points –

Maria   [*interrupting*] – That if one breaks, the other will take
the strain. Or, if both break, your breeches will fall down . . .

Feste   [*as one jester to another*] Apt, indeed. Very apt. Well,
off you go. If Sir Toby would give up drinking you'd be as
witty a young wench as any in Illyria . . .

Maria   [*blushing at the hint of marriage*] That's enough of
that, you rogue! Here comes my lady. You'd better have a
good excuse!

[*She goes*]

Feste   [*touching his hands together as if in prayer*] If it be thy
will, oh Wit, may my fooling be in good form. Clowns who
think they're gifted with wit usually prove to be fools. As I
know I'm not witty, that makes me a wise man. What does
Quinapulus say? [*He has made the name up*]: 'Better a witty
fool than a foolish wit'.

45

[*Enter* **Olivia, Malvolio,** *and* **Attendants**]

God bless thee, lady!

Olivia   Take the fool away.

Feste   Do you not hear, fellows? Take away the lady.

35 **Olivia**   Go to, you're a dry fool; I'll no more of you; besides
you grow dishonest.

Feste   Two faults, madonna, that drink and good counsel will
amend; for give the dry fool drink, then is the fool not dry;
bid the dishonest man mend himself; if he mend, he is no
40   longer dishonest; if he cannot, let the botcher mend him.
Anything that's mended is but patched; virtue that
transgresses is but patched with sin; and sin that amends is
but patched with virtue. If that this simple syllogism will
serve, so; if it will not, what remedy? As there is no true
45   cuckold but calamity, so beauty's a flower. The lady bade
take away the fool; therefore, I say again, take her away.

Olivia   Sir, I bade them take away you.

Feste   Misprision in the highest degree! Lady, *cucullus non
facit monachum:* that's as much to say as I wear not motley in
50   my brain. Good madonna, give me leave to prove you a fool.

Olivia   Can you do it?

Feste   Dexteriously, good madonna.

Olivio   Make your proof.

Feste   I must catechize you for it, madonna; good my mouse of
55   virtue, answer me.

[**Olivia** *enters, followed by her solemn steward* **Malvolio** *and* **Attendants**]

God bless you, lady!

Olivia   [*with a weary gesture*] Take the fool away.

Feste   [*to the* **Attendants**] Didn't you hear, fellows? Take the lady away!

Olivia   [*to* **Feste***; she is in no mood for jokes*] Don't talk rubbish. You have a dry sort of wit. I've had enough of you. Besides, you're becoming dishonest.

Feste   Two faults, madam, that drink and good advice will put right. Give the dry fool drink – then he isn't a dry fool any more. Order the dishonest man to mend his ways: and if he does, he stops being dishonest. If he can't mend his ways, let a cheap tailor mend him. Anything that is mended is patched. Virtue that goes wrong is patched with sin. Sin that mends its ways is patched with virtue. If this simple logic is acceptable, fine. If it isn't, what can be done about it? Learn from misfortune: beauty fades like a flower. The lady ordered the fool to be taken away; therefore, I say again: take her away!

Olivia   Sir, I ordered them to take *you* away.

Feste   The height of mockery! Lady, 'a hood doesn't make a monk'. In other words, don't be deceived by my jester's clothes: my *brain* isn't clad in motley. My lady, give me permission to prove that you are a fool.

Olivia   Can you do it?

Feste   With the greatest of ease, my lady.

Olivia   Make your proof . . .

Feste   I must cross-question you for it, my lady. My little virtuous mouse must answer me.

Olivia Well, sir, for want of other idleness, I'll bide your proof.

Feste Good madonna, why mournest thou?

Olivia Good fool, for my brother's death.

60 **Feste** I think his soul is in hell, madonna.

Olivia I know his soul is in heaven, fool.

Feste The more fool, madonna, to mourn for your brother's soul being in heaven. Take away the fool, gentlemen.

Olivia What think you of this fool, Malvolio? Doth he not
65 mend?

Malvolio Yes; and shall do till the pangs of death shake him; infirmity, that decays the wise, doth ever make the better fool.

Feste God send you, sir, a speedy infirmity, for the better
70 increasing your folly! Sir Toby will be sworn that I am no fox, but he will not pass his word for two pence that you are no fool.

Olivia How say you to that, Malvolio?

Malvolio I marvel your ladyship takes delight in such a
75 barren rascal; I saw him put down the other day with an ordinary fool that has no more brain than a stone. Look you now, he's out of his guard already; unless you laugh and minister occasion to him, he is gagged. I protest, I take these wise men, that crow so at these set kind of fools, no better
80 than the fools' zanies.

Olivia O, you are sick of self-love, Malvolio, and taste with a distempered appetite. To be generous, guiltless, and of free disposition, is to take those things for bird-bolts that you deem cannon-bullets. There is no slander in an allowed fool,

Olivia   Well, sir, since I've nothing better to do, I'll endure
listening to your proof.

Feste   My lady, why are you in mourning?

Olivia   Good fool, for my brother's death.

Feste   I think his soul is in hell, my lady.

Olivia   I know his soul is in heaven, fool.

Feste   The more fool my lady, to mourn for your brother's soul
being in heaven! [*To the* **Attendants**] Take away the fool,
gentlemen!

Olivia   [*to* **Malvolio**] What do you think of this fool, Malvolio?
Isn't he improving?

Malvolio   [*with typical disdain*] Yes, and he'll continue to, till
he's in his death throes. Old age, which makes wise men
deteriorate, always does make fools more foolish.

Feste   [*bowing*] God send you sir, a swift old age, to increase
your folly all the more. Sir Toby will swear I'm no sharp-wit;
but he wouldn't take tuppence for swearing that you are not
a fool.

Olivia   What do you say to that, Malvolio!

Malvolio   I'm astonished that your ladyship gains any pleasure
from such an empty-headed rascal. I saw him outclassed the
other day by an ordinary fool who had no more brains than a
stone. [**Feste** *reacts*] Look at him: he's off-balance already.
Unless you laugh and give him an opening, he dries up.
Really, I regard these wise men who guffaw so loudly at
these predictable fools, as no better than the fools' puppets.

Olivia   Oh, you think too highly of yourself, Malvolio, and your
opinion is sourly prejudiced. To be generous, tolerant and
kindly, one should regard as mere pellets what you are
calling cannon-balls. There's nothing slanderous in a fool

49

85   though he do nothing but rail; nor no railing in a known
      discreet man, though he do nothing but reprove.

Feste   Now, Mercury endue thee with leasing, for thou
      speakest well of fools!

[*Enter* **Maria**]

Maria   Madam, there is at the gate a young gentleman much
90   desires to speak with you.

Olivia   From the Count Orsino, is it?

Maria   I know not, madam; 'tis a fair young man, and well
      attended.

Olivia   Who of my people hold him in delay?

95 **Maria**   Sir Toby, madam, your kinsman.

Olivia   Fetch him off, I pray you; he speaks nothing but
      madman. Fie on him!

[*Exit* **Maria**]

      Go you, Malvolio; if it be a suit from the count, I am sick or
      not at home, what you will to dismiss it.

[*Exit* **Malvolio**]

100   Now you see, sir, how your fooling grows old, and people
      dislike it.

Feste   Thou hast spoke for us, madonna, as if thy eldest son
      should be a fool; whose skull Jove cram with brains! for here
      he comes, one of thy kin has a most weak *pia mater*.

[*Enter* **Sir Toby Belch**]

who's licensed to be cheeky, even if all he does is hurl
abuse. There's nothing abusive in a man recognized for his
discretion, even if all he does is scold.

Feste   [*cheering up*] May the God of Liars, Mercury, make you
a good fibber, 'cos you speak well of fools!

[**Maria** *returns*]

Maria   Madam, there is a young gentleman at the gate who
very much wants to speak with you.

Olivia   From the Count Orsino, is he?

Maria   I don't know, madam. He's a nice young man with
several attendants with him.

Olivia   Which of my people is keeping him waiting?

Maria   Sir Toby, madam, your relative.

Olivia   Fetch him away, please, will you? He talks like a
lunatic. Shame on him!

[**Maria** *goes*]

You go, Malvolio. If it's a proposal from the Count, say I'm
sick, or not at home, or whatever you please to get rid of it.

[**Malvolio** *leaves*]

[*to* **Feste**]

Now you see, sir, how your fooling grows tedious, and
people dislike it.

Feste   You have spoken up for us jesters, my lady, as though
your eldest son was a fool. May God cram his skull full of
brains – because here comes one of your relatives whose
grey matter isn't up to standard.

[**Sir Toby Belch** *enters; he has been drinking*]

105 **Olivia**   By mine honour, half drunk! What is he at the gate,
cousin?

Sir Toby   A gentleman.

Olivia   A gentleman! What gentleman?

Sir Toby   'Tis a gentleman here – a plague o' these pickle-
110   herring! How now, sot!

Feste   Good Sir Toby!

Olivia   Cousin, cousin, how have you come so early by this
lethargy?

Sir Toby   Lechery! I defy lechery. There's one at the gate.

115 **Olivia**   Ay, marry; what is he?

Sir Toby   Let him be the devil, an he will, I care not; give me
faith, say I. Well, it's all one.

[*Exit*]

Olivia   What's a drunken man like, fool?

Feste   Like a drowned man, a fool, and a madman; one
120   draught above heat makes him a fool, the second mads him,
and a third drowns him.

Olivia   Go thou and seek the crowner, and let him sit o' my
coz; for he's in the third degree of drink, he's drowned; go,
look after him.

125 **Feste**   He is but mad yet, madonna; and the fool shall look to
the madman.

[*Exit*]

Olivia   Upon my honour, he's half drunk. [*To* **Sir Toby**] What sort of person is at the gate, cousin?

Sir Toby   A gentleman.

Olivia   A gentleman? What gentleman?

Sir Toby   There's a gentleman here – [*He stops and belches loudly*] Damn these pickled herrings! [*He sees* **Feste**] Greetings, clot!

Feste   Dear Sir Toby!

Olivia   Cousin, cousin, how do you come to have this dullness, this lethargy, so early?

Sir Toby   [*mishearing*] Lechery! I defy lechery! There's somebody at the gate.

Olivia   Yes, indeed. What sort of man is he?

Sir Toby   He can be the devil if he wants to be, I don't care. Give me faith, I say. Well, it's all the same to me.

[*He totters off*]

Olivia   What's a drunken man like, fool?

Feste   Like a drowned man, a fool, and a madman. One drink too many makes him foolish; the second makes him mad; and the third drowns him.

Olivia   Go and find the coroner, and let him consider the case of my cousin. He's in the third degree of drink; he's drowned. Go and look after him.

Feste   He's only at the mad stage yet, my lady. The fool will look after the madman.

[*He leaves*]

[*Enter* **Malvolio**]

Malvolio   Madam, yond young fellow swears he will speak
with you. I told him you were sick; he takes on him to
understand so much, and therefore comes to speak with you.
130   I told him you were asleep; he seems to have a foreknowledge
of that too, and therefore comes to speak with you. What is
to be said to him, lady? He's fortified against any denial.

Olivia   Tell him he shall not speak with me.

Malvolio   Has been told so; and he says he'll stand at your
135   door like a sheriff's post, and be the supporter to a bench,
but he'll speak with you.

Olivia   What kind o' man is he?

Malvolio   Why, of mankind.

Olivia   What manner of man?

140   **Malvolio**   Of very ill manner; he'll speak with you, will you
or no.

Olivia   Of what personage and years is he?

Malvolio   Not yet old enough for a man, nor young enough
for a boy; as a squash is before 'tis a peascod, or a codling
145   when 'tis almost an apple; 'tis with him in standing water,
between boy and man. He is very well-favoured, and he
speaks very shrewishly; one would think his mother's milk
were scarce out of him.

Olivia   Let him approach. Call in my gentlewoman.

150   **Malvolio**   Gentlewoman, my lady calls.

[*Exit*]

[*Enter* **Maria**]

[**Malvolio** *returns*]

Malvolio   Madam, the young fellow there insists on speaking
to you. I told him you were sick. He affects to know that
already, so he therefore comes to speak to you. I told him
you were asleep. He seems to have a foreknowledge of that,
too, and therefore comes to speak to you. What is to be said
to him, my lady? He's proof against all excuses.

Olivia   Tell him he shall not speak to me.

Malvolio   He's been told so. He says he'll stand at your door
like a flagpole, or prop up a bench, but he will speak to you.

Olivia   What kind of man is he?

Malvolio   Why, of the human race . . .

Olivia   What *type* of man?

Malvolio   Very objectionable. He'll speak to you whether you
wish it or not.

Olivia   What's his demeanour, and how old is he?

Malvolio   Not old enough to be a man, nor young enough to be
a boy; like a pea-pod before it's full size, or a pippin is before
it's an apple. With him it's like the sea between tides: he's
between boy and man. He's very handsome, and he speaks
very sharply. One would think he'd only just been weaned.

Olivia   Let him come in. Call in my maidservant.

Malvolio   Maid! My lady wants you.

[*He goes*]

[**Maria** *enters*]

55

Olivia   Give me my veil; come, throw it o'er my face. We'll
once more hear Orsino's embassy.

[*Enter* **Viola** *and* **Attendants**]

Viola   The honourable lady of the house, which is she?

Olivia   Speak to me; I shall answer for her. Your will?

155   **Viola**   Most radiant, exquisite, and unmatchable beauty – I
pray you, tell me if this be the lady of the house, for I never
saw her. I would be loath to cast away my speech; for besides
that it is excellently well penned, I have taken great pains to
con it. Good beauties, let me sustain no scorn; I am very
160   comptible, even to the least sinister usage.

Olivia   Whence came you, sir?

Viola   I can say little more than I have studied, and that
question's out of my part. Good gentle one, give me modest
assurance if you be the lady of the house, that I may proceed
165   in my speech.

Olivia   Are you a comedian?

Viola   No, my profound heart; and yet, by the very fangs of
malice I swear I am not that I play. Are you the lady of the
house?

170   **Olivia**   If I do not usurp myself, I am.

Viola   Most certain, if you are she, you do usurp yourself; for
what is yours to bestow is not yours to reserve. But this is
from my commission; I will on with my speech in your
praise, and then show you the heart of my message.

Olivia   Give me my veil; throw it over my face. We'll hear
Orsino's message once again.

[**Viola** *and* **Attendants** *enter*]

Viola   The honourable lady of the house: which is she?

Olivia   Speak to me. I'll answer for her. What is it you want?

Viola   [*starting her prepared speech*] Most radiant, exquisite
and unmatchable beauty . . . [*she stops and looks round*]
Please, do tell me if this is the lady of the house, because
I've never seen her. I'd hate to waste my speech, because
apart from the fact that it's excellently written, I've worked
hard to learn it by heart. [**Olivia**'s **attendants** *cannot
suppress a laugh*] Good people, do not laugh at me: I take
offence easily, even to the slightest impoliteness.

Olivia   Where have you come from, sir?

Viola   I can say little more than I've learned, and that question
isn't in my script. Gentle madam, give me some small
indication that you really are the lady of the house, so that I
can proceed with my speech.

Olivia   Are you an actor?

Viola   No, bless me, and yet, in spite of wicked rumours, I
swear I'm not what I appear to be. Are you the lady of the
house?

Olivia   Unless I do myself an injustice, I am.

Viola   Certainly, if you are the lady of the house, you *are* doing
yourself an injustice because [*hinting at* **Olivia**'s *hand in
marriage*] what is yours to give away isn't yours to withhold.
But this isn't part of my instructions. I'll carry on with my
speech in your praise, then I'll get to the main part of my
message.

175 **Olivia**   Come to what is important in't; I forgive you the
praise.

Viola   Alas! I took great pains to study it, and 'tis poetical.

Olivia   It is the more like to be feigned; I pray you keep it in. I
heard you were saucy at my gates, and allowed your
180 approach, rather to wonder at you than to hear you. If you
be not mad, be gone; if you have reason, be brief; 'tis not that
time of moon with me to make one in so skipping a dialogue.

Maria   Will you hoist sail, sir? here lies your way.

Viola   No, good swabber; I am to hull here a little longer.
185 Some mollification for your giant, sweet lady.

Olivia   Tell me your mind.

Viola   I am a messenger.

Olivia   Sure, you have some hideous matter to deliver, when
the courtesy of it is so fearful. Speak your office.

190 **Viola**   It alone concerns your ear. I bring no overture of war,
no taxation of homage; I hold the olive in my hand; my words
are as full of peace as matter.

Olivia   Yet you began rudely. What are you? What would
you?

195 **Viola**   The rudeness that hath appeared in me have I learned
from my entertainment. What I am, and what I would, are as
secret as maidenhead; to your ears, divinity; to any other's,
profanation.

Olivia   Give us the place alone; we will hear this divinity.

[*Exeunt* **Maria** *and* **Attendants**

200 Now, sir; what is your text?

Olivia   Get to the important bit: I'll let you off the praise.

Viola   Alas, I took great pains to learn it, and it's poetical . . .

Olivia   It's all the more likely to be insincere. Keep it to yourself, do. I heard you were cheeky at my gates and allowed you in more to wonder at you than to hear you. If you're mad, be off with you. If you're sane, be brief. I'm not in the mood to take part in such a silly conversation.

Maria   Will you hoist your sails, sir? [*Pointing to the door*] There's your route . . .

Viola   [*to* **Maria**, *carrying on the seafaring image*] No, good deckhand, I've got to lie at anchor here a little longer. [*To* **Olivia**] Keep your giant off me, sweet lady. [**Maria** *is, in fact, quite small*]

Olivia   Say what's on your mind.

Viola   I am a messenger.

Olivia   You must surely have some dreadful news to deliver, when the formalities are so mind-boggling. Say what you have to say.

Viola   It's very personal. I bring you no declaration of war, no demands for protection-money. I hold an olive branch in my hand; my words are those of peace, not argument.

Olivia   Yet you began impolitely. What are you? What do you want?

Viola   My rudeness was the result of the way I was received. What I am, and what I want, are as secret as virginity. To your ears: divine. To any other's: profane.

Olivia   [*gesturing to her* **Attendants**] Leave us alone. I'll hear this 'divinity'.

[**Maria** *and the* **Attendants** *leave*]

Now, sir. What's your sermon?

Viola   Most sweet lady –

Olivia   A comfortable doctrine, and much may be said of it.
Where lies your text?

Viola   In Orsino's bosom.

205 **Olivia**   In his bosom! In what chapter of his bosom?

Viola   To answer by the method, in the first of his heart.

Olivia   O! I have read it; it is heresy. Have you no more to
say?

Viola   Good madam, let me see your face.

210 **Olivia**   Have you any commission from your lord to negotiate
with my face? You are now out of your text; but we will draw
the curtain and show you the picture. (*Unveiling*) Look you,
sir; such a one I was this present; is't not well done?

Viola   Excellently done, if God did all.

215 **Olivia**   'Tis in grain, sir; 'twill endure wind and weather.

Viola   'Tis beauty truly blent, whose red and white
Nature's own sweet and cunning hand laid on;
Lady, you are the cruell'st she alive,
If you will lead these graces to the grave
220 And leave the world no copy.

Olivia   O, sir, I will not be so hard-hearted! I will give out
divers schedules of my beauty; it shall be inventoried, and
every particle and utensil labelled to my will, as, Item, Two
lips indifferent red; Item, Two grey eyes with lids to them;
225 Item, One neck, one chin, and so forth. Were you sent hither
to praise me?

Viola   I see you what you are; you are too proud;
But, if you were the devil, you are fair.
My lord and master loves you; O! such love

Viola Most sweet lady –

Olivia [*drily*] A safe theological base, and there's a great deal to be said for it. Where does your text come from?

Viola Orsino's heart.

Olivia His heart! In what chapter of his heart?

Viola To answer in religious style: Chapter One of his heart.

Olivia Oh, I've read it. It's heresy. Have you anything else to say?

Viola Good madam: let me see your face.

Olivia Have you been commissioned by your master to negotiate with my face? You've left your text. But we'll draw the curtain and show you the picture. [*She lifts her veil*] Look, sir: this is how I looked just now. Isn't it a good likeness?

Viola Excellently done – if it's all God's work!

Olivia It's fixed, sir; it will endure wind and weather.

Viola It is beauty well blended: the reds and whites, the work of Nature's sweet and talented hand. Lady, you are the cruellest woman living if you will take these gifts to the grave, and leave the world no copy.

Olivia Oh, sir, I won't be so hard-hearted! I'll publish various catalogues of my beauty. It will be inventoried, and every detail and piece of equipment labelled according to my wishes. For example, Item: two lips, fairly red. Item: two grey eyes with lids to them. Item: one neck, one chin, and so forth. Were you sent here to make a valuation?

Viola I see what you are! You are too proud! But even if you were the devil, I couldn't deny you are beautiful. My lord and master loves you. Such love could only be recompensed if

61

230   Could be but recompensed, though you were crowned
        The nonpareil of beauty.

Olivia   How does he love me?

Viola   With adorations, fertile tears,
        With groans that thunder love, with sighs of fire.

Olivia   Your lord does know my mind; I cannot love him;
235   Yet I suppose him virtuous, know him noble,
        Of great estate, of fresh and stainless youth;
        In voices well divulged, free, learned, and valiant;
        And in dimension and the shape of nature
        A gracious person; but yet I cannot love him.
240   He might have took his answer long ago.

Viola   If I did love you in my master's flame,
        With such a suffering, such a deadly life,
        In your denial I would find no sense;
        I would not understand it.

Olivia   Why, what would you?

245 **Viola**   Make me a willow cabin at your gate,
        And call upon my soul within the house;
        Write loyal cantons of contemned love,
        And sing them loud even in the dead of night;
        Holla your name to the reverberate hills,
250   And make the babbling gossip of the air
        Cry out 'Olivia!' O, you should not rest
        Between the elements of air and earth
        But you should pity me!

Olivia   You might do much. What is your parentage?

255 **Viola**   Above my fortunes, yet my state is well:
        I am a gentleman.

Olivia   Get you to your lord;
        I cannot love him. Let him send no more,

you were crowned as the most beautiful woman in the world.

Olivia How does he love me?

Viola Adoringly; with copious tears; with groans that thunder out their love; with passionate sighs . . .

Olivia Your lord knows my feelings: I cannot love him. But I take his virtue for granted; know him to be noble; very rich; of fresh and uncorrupted youth; well spoken of; liberal, learned and valiant; a gracious person in shape and figure. But nevertheless I cannot love him. He should have accepted his answer long ago.

Viola If I loved you with the ardour of my master, with such suffering, with such wretchedness, I'd make no sense of your rejection. I wouldn't understand it.

Olivia Why, what would you do?

Viola I'd make a shelter underneath the willow at your gate, and call upon my loved one who lives inside the house. I'd write devoted songs of hopeless love, and sing them loudly in the middle of the night. I'd shout your name to the echoing hills, and make the reverberations cry out 'Olivia!' Oh, you couldn't live on this earth and not feel pity for me!

Olivia In your case, you might succeed. What is your rank?

Viola Above my present fortune, but I am well-bred. I am a gentleman.

Olivia Return to your lord. I can't love him. Tell him to send no

Unless, perchance, you come to me again,
To tell me how he takes it. Fare you well;
260   I thank you for your pains; spend this for me.

Viola   I am no fee'd post, lady; keep your purse;
My master, not myself, lacks recompense.
Love make his heart of flint that you shall love,
And let your fervour, like my master's, be
265   Placed in contempt! Farewell, fair cruelty.

                                                      [Exit]

Olivia   'What is your parentage?'
'Above my fortunes, yet my state is well;
I am a gentleman.' I'll be sworn thou art;
Thy tongue, thy face, thy limbs, actions, and spirit,
270   Do give thee five-fold blazon. Not too fast; soft! soft! –
Unless the master were the man. Now now!
Even so quickly may one catch the plague?
Methinks I feel this youth's perfections,
With an invisible and subtle stealth
275   To creep in at mine eyes. Well, let it be.
What, ho! Malvolio!

    [Enter **Malvolio**]

Malvolio   Here, madam, at your service.

Olivia   Run after that same peevish messenger,
The county's man; he left this ring behind him,
Would I or not; tell him I'll none of it.
280   Desire him not to flatter with his lord,
Nor hold him up with hopes; I am not for him.
If that the youth will come this way tomorrow,
I'll give him reasons for 't. Hie thee, Malvolio.

more messages – unless, perhaps, *you* come to me again.
Tell me how he takes it. Goodbye. I thank you for the trouble
you have taken. [*She gives* **Viola** *a purse of money*] Spend
this for me.

Viola   I'm no paid messenger, lady. Keep your purse. It's my
master, not myself, who lacks reward. May the man you
love have a heart of stone, and may your ardour, like my
master's, be treated with contempt! Farewell, you cruel
beauty!

[**Viola** *goes*]

Olivia   What is your rank? 'Above my present fortune, but I am
well-bred: I am a gentleman'. I'll swear an oath you are!
Your voice, your face, your limbs, actions and spirit bespeak
a five-star pedigree. [*She thinks*] Not too fast . . . softly,
softly . . . Now if the master were the man . . . What then?
Can one fall in love so quickly? I suspect this youth's fine
qualities are subtly and invisibly creeping their way in, via my
eyes. Well, so be it. [*She calls*] Hello, there! Malvolio! [*She
takes a ring from her finger*]

[**Malvolio** *returns*]

Malvolio   Here madam, at your service.

Olivia   Run after that rude messenger fellow, the Count's
man. [*She hands him a ring*] He left this ring behind him,
despite what I said. Tell him I won't have it. Tell him not to
mince matters with his lord, nor give him false hope. I'm not
for him. Should the youth come this way tomorrow, I'll give
him my reasons. Hurry, Malvolio.

Malvolio   Madam, I will.

[*Exit*]

285 **Olivia**   I do I know not what, and fear to find
         Mine eye too great a flatterer for my mind.
         Fate, show thy force; ourselves we do not owe;
         What is decreed must be, and be this so.

[*Exit*]

Malvolio   Madam, I will.

[*He leaves in the same stately fashion as he entered*]

Olivia   I don't entirely know what I'm doing, and fear my eyes may be turning my head. Fate: show your power! We are not our own masters. What must be, must be: this is no exception.

Act two

Scene 1

The Sea-coast. Enter **Antonio** *and* **Sebastian**

Antonio   Will you stay no longer, nor will you not that I go
with you?

Sebastian   By your patience, no. My stars shine darkly over
me; the malignancy of my fate might, perhaps, distemper
5   yours; therefore I shall crave of you your leave that I may
bear my evils alone. It were a bad recompense for your love,
to lay any of them on you.

Antonio   Let me yet know of you whither you are bound.

Sebastian   No, sooth, sir; my determinate voyage is mere
10   extravagancy. But I perceive in you so excellent a touch of
modesty, that you will not extort from me what I am willing
to keep in; therefore it charges me in manners the rather to
express myself. You must know of me then, Antonio, my
name is Sebastian, which I called Roderigo. My father was
15   that Sebastian of Messaline, whom I know you have heard
of. He left behind him myself and a sister, both born in an
hour; if the heavens had been pleased, would we had so
ended! But you, sir, altered that; for some hour before you
took me from the breach of the sea was my sister drowned.

20 **Antonio**   Alas the day!

Sebastian   A lady, sir, though it was said she much resembled
me, was yet of many accounted beautiful; but, though I could
not with such estimable wonder overfar believe that, yet thus
far I will boldly publish her; she bore a mind that Envy could

Act two

Scene 1

The sea-coast of Illyria. Enter **Antonio** [*a sea-captain*] *and* **Sebastian**, *Viola's brother*

Antonio Won't you stay longer? Can't I go with you?

Sebastian Forgive me, no. I'm not in luck these days, and my ill-fate might, perhaps, affect yours. So may I ask you to let me bear my misfortunes alone? It would be poor payment for your love to pass any of them over to you.

Antonio At least tell me where you are going.

Sebastian No, really, sir. Where I'm going is quite arbitrary. *absolute* And I'm sure you are too polite to extort information from me that I'd rather keep to myself. So good manners equally oblige me to tell you what I can. I'll tell you, therefore, Antonio, that my real name is Sebastian, though I said I was Roderigo. My father was Sebastian of Messaline: I know you will have heard of him. He left behind him myself and a twin sister; we were born within an hour of each other. If Heaven had been willing, would we had died similarly; but you, sir, changed that. About an hour before you rescued me at the shore-line, my sister was drowned.

Antonio How awful!

Sebastian She was a lady, sir, who though it was said she greatly resembled me, was nonetheless considered beautiful. Though I couldn't, without overstretching my imagination, go so far as to believe that, I'll go this far in proclaiming her qualities: her mind was certainly beautiful, which not even Envy itself could deny. She has already been

69

25   not but call fair. She is drowned already, sir, with salt water,
     though I seem to drown her remembrance again with more.

Antonio   Pardon me, sir, your bad entertainment.

Sebastian   O good Antonio! forgive me your trouble.

Antonio   If you will not murder me for my love, let me be
30   your servant.

Sebastian   If you will not undo what you have done, that is,
     kill him whom you have recovered, desire it not. Fare ye
     well at once; my bosom is full of kindness; and I am yet so
     near the manners of my mother that upon the least occasion
35   more mine eyes will tell tales of me. I am bound to the
     Count Orsino's court; farewell.

[*Exit*]

Antonio   The gentleness of all the gods go with thee!
     I have many enemies in Orsino's court,
     Else would I very shortly see thee there;
40   But, come what may, I do adore thee so,
     That danger shall seem sport, and I will go.

[*Exit*]

Scene 2

A Street. Enter **Viola; Malvolio** *following*

Malvolio   Were you not even now with the Countess Olivia?

Viola   Even now, sir; on a moderate pace I have since arrived
     but hither.

ACT TWO   Scene 1

drowned in salt water, though I seem to drown her memory
in more. (*He chokes back a tear*)

Antonio   [*realizing* **Sebastian** *is a gentleman*] Excuse my
humble hospitality, sir.

Sebastian   Oh, good Antonio: forgive me the trouble I've put
you to.

Antonio   If you don't want me to die from pining after you, let
me be your servant!

Sebastian   Unless you want to undo what you have
done – that is, kill the man you have just rescued – don't
ask that. Right now, goodbye. My heart is full of tender
feelings for you, and I'm still so much my mother's son that
at the least provocation my eyes will betray my emotions yet
again. I'm going to the court of Count Orsino. Farewell.

[*He goes, quickly*]

Antonio   May the gods protect you kindly! I have many
enemies in Orsino's court or else I'd very soon see you
there. [*He turns to go, then stops to think again*] But
whatever the consequences I'm so fond of you that danger
will seem like fun: so I will go!

Scene 2

A street. Enter **Viola**, *followed by* **Malvolio**

Malvolio   Were you not with the Countess Olivia just now?

Viola   Just this minute, sir. Walking fairly slowly, I've just
reached here.

71

Malvolio   She returns this ring to you, sir; you might have
5   saved me my pains, to have taken it away yourself. She adds,
moreover, that you should put your lord into a desperate
assurance she will none of him. And one thing more: that
you be never so hardy to come again in his affairs, unless it
be to report your lord's taking of this. Receive it so.

10 **Viola**   She took the ring of me; I'll none of it.

Malvolio   Come, sir, you peevishly threw it to her; and her
will is it should be so returned; if it be worth stooping for,
there it lies in your eye; if not, be it his that finds it.

[*Exit*]

Viola   I left no ring with her; what means this lady?
15   Fortune forbid my outside have not charmed her!
She made good view of me; indeed so much
That sure methought her eyes had lost her tongue,
For she did speak in starts distractedly.
She loves me, sure; the cunning of her passion
20   Invites me in this churlish messenger.
None of my lord's ring! Why, he sent her none.
I am the man; if it be so, as 'tis,
Poor lady, she were better love a dream.
Disguise, I see thou art a wickedness
25   Wherein the pregnant enemy does much.
How easy is it for the proper-false
In women's waxen hearts to set their forms!
Alas! our frailty is the cause, not we,
For such as we are made of, such we be.
30   How will this fadge? My master loves her dearly;

Malvolio [*holding out Olivia's ring between extended finger and thumb*] She returns this ring to you, sir. You might have saved me the trouble by taking it away yourself. She adds, moreover, that you should make it absolutely clear to your master that she'll have nothing to do with him. And one thing more: you must never be so bold as to come again on his affairs, unless it be to report that your lord has taken this back. Have it back thus. [*He throws the ring on the ground*]

Viola [*pausing to think, then summing the situation up*] She took the ring from me. I don't want it now.

Malvolio Come, sir. You rudely threw it to her, and her decision is that it should be returned in the same way. If it's worth stooping for, there it lies where you can see it. If not, it belongs to whoever finds it.

[*He takes himself off*]

Viola I didn't leave a ring with her. What does the lady mean? Heaven forbid she hasn't taken a fancy to my appearance! She looked me over a lot: indeed, so much so that I thought her eyes had made her tongue-tied, because she spoke in fits and starts, excitedly. She loves me, that's for sure. It's cunning brought about by passion that has led her to invite me back again as the rude messenger. [*Scornfully*] She won't have my lord's ring! [*She chuckles to herself*] Why, he didn't send her one! I'm her man. If it's what it seems, poor lady, she might as well be in love with a dream! Disguise, I realize you are a form of wickedness giving ample scope to the devil and his work. How easy it is for philanderers to melt the hearts of susceptible women. Alas, it's our weakness that's the cause, not ourselves. What we are made of, that we must be. [*She thinks*] How will this all end? My master loves her dearly, and I, poor devil, am

And I, poor monster, fond as much on him;
And she, mistaken, seems to dote on me.
What will become of this? As I am man,
My state is desperate for my master's love;
35   As I am woman – now alas the day! –
What thriftless sighs shall poor Olivia breathe!
O time, thou must untangle this, not I;
It is too hard a knot for me to untie.

[*Exit*]

Scene 3

Olivia's House. Enter **Sir Toby Belch** *and* **Sir Andrew Aguecheek**

Sir Toby   Approach, Sir Andrew: not to be a-bed after
midnight is to be up betimes; and *diluculo surgere*, thou
knowest –

Sir Andrew   Nay, by my troth, I know not; but I know, to be
5   up late is to be up late.

Sir Toby   A false conclusion; I hate it as an unfilled can. To
be up after midnight, and to go to bed then, is early; so that
to go to bed after midnight is to go to bed betimes. Does not
our life consist of the four elements?

10 **Sir Andrew**   Faith, so they say; but I think it rather consists of
eating and drinking.

equally fond of him; and she, not knowing, seems to dote on
me. What will be the outcome? As a man, I stand no chance
of my master's love. As I'm a woman – alas the day I
ceased to be! – what futile sighs shall poor Olivia breathe!
[*She shakes her head*] Oh, time must disentangle this,
not me. It's far too hard a knot for me to untie!

Scene 3

A room in Olivia's house. Enter **Sir Toby Belch** *and* **Sir
Andrew Aguecheek**. *They are both drunk*

Sir Toby   Come on, Sir Andrew: not to be in bed after
midnight is to be up early. As the Latin tag says, 'To get up
at daybreak . . .' you know. [*He thinks* **Sir Andrew** *is
educated enough to add 'is good for your health'*]

Sir Andrew   No, actually, I don't know. But I do know that to
be up late is – to be up late.

Sir Toby   That's false logic. I hate it [*he begins to drink from
his tankard, but puts it down*] like an empty pot. To be up
after midnight, and to go to bed then, is early . . . so that to
go to bed after midnight is to go to bed early. [*They consider
this solemnly*] Doesn't our life consist of the four elements
of fire, earth, air and water?

Sir Andrew   Faith, so they say. But I think it really consists of
eating and drinking.

Sir Toby   Thou'rt a scholar; let us therefore eat and drink.
Marian, I say! a stoup of wine!

[*Enter* **Feste**]

Sir Andrew   Here comes the fool, i' faith.

15 **Feste**   How now, my hearts! Did you never see the picture of
'we three'?

Sir Toby   Welcome, ass. Now let's have a catch.

Sir Andrew   By my troth, the fool has an excellent breast. I
had rather than forty shillings I had such a leg, and so sweet
20   a breath to sing, as the fool has. [*To* **Feste**] In sooth, thou
wast in very gracious fooling last night, when thou spokest
of Pigrogromitus, of the Vapians passing the equinoctial of
Queubus; 'twas very good, i' faith. I sent thee sixpence for
thy leman; hadst it?

25 **Feste**   I did impeticos thy gratillity, for Malvolio's nose is no
whipstock; my lady has a white hand, and the Myrmidons are
no bottle-ale houses.

Sir Andrew   Excellent! Why, this is the best fooling, when all
is done. Now, a song.

30 **Sir Toby**   Come on; there is sixpence for you; let's have a song.

Sir Andrew   There's a testril of me too; if one knight give a –

Sir Toby   You are a scholar! Let us therefore eat and drink.
[*Calling*] Maria, I say! A flagon of wine!

[**Feste** *enters*]

Sir Andrew   Here comes the fool indeed!

Feste   How goes it, my hearties? [*He puts his arms round
them both*] Have you never seen the picture of 'we three'?
[*He's referring to inn signs with two wooden heads painted
on them: the third is the onlooker*]

Sir Toby   Welcome, ass. Now let's sing a catch! [*They need
three voices for this kind of song*]

Sir ~~Toby~~ ANDREW   Upon my word, the fool has an excellent voice. I'd
rather have the fool's shapely leg and his sweet breath to
sing with, than forty shillings. [*To Feste*] Honestly, you were
in great form last night when you spoke of 'Pigrogromitus',
and of 'the Vapians passing the equinoctial of Queubus'.
[**Feste** *is fond of learned double-talk*] It was very good
indeed. I sent you sixpence for your sweetheart. Did you get
it?

Feste   [*giving* **Sir Andrew** *value for his money*] I impeticossed
your gratillity, 'cos Malvolio's nose is long, my lady is of the
upper classes, and you can't get cheap ale at 'The
Myrmidons'.

Sir Andrew   [*delighted at the mixture of sense and nonsense*]
Excellent! Why this is top-class fooling, all things
considered. Now for a song!

Sir Toby   [*tipping* **Feste**] Come on; there's sixpence for you.
Let's have a song.

Sir Andrew   There's a tanner from me, too. If one knight
gives a –

Feste   Would you have a love-song, or a song of good life?

Sir Toby   A love-song, a love-song.

Sir Andrew   Ay, ay; I care not for good life.

35 **Feste**   [*Singing*]   *O mistress mine! where are you roaming?*
O stay and hear! your true love's coming,
That can sing both high and low.
Trip no further, pretty sweeting;
Journeys end in lovers meeting,
40   *Every wise man's son doth know.*

Sir Andrew   Excellent good, i' faith.

Sir Toby   Good, good.

Feste   [*Singing*]   *What is love? 'Tis not hereafter;*
Present mirth hath present laughter;
45   *What's to come is still unsure.*
In delay there lies no plenty;
Then come kiss me, sweet-and-twenty,
Youth's a stuff will not endure.

Sir Andrew   A mellifluous voice, as I am true knight.

50 **Sir Toby**   A contagious breath.

Sir Andrew   Very sweet and contagious, i' faith.

Sir Toby   To hear by the nose, it is dulcet in contagion. But
shall we make the welkin dance indeed? Shall we rouse the
night-owl in a catch that will draw three souls out of one
55   weaver? Shall we do that?

Sir Andrew   An you love me, let's do 't; I am dog at a catch.

Feste   By'r lady, sir, and some dogs will catch well.

Feste [*interrupting*] Do you want a love-song, or a song about how good life is?

Sir Toby A love-song, a love-song!

Sir Andrew Yes, yes. I don't care for the good life.

Feste [*Singing as he plays on his stringed instrument*]
Oh, mistress mine, where are you roaming?
Oh, stay and hear! Your true love's coming.
  That can sing both high and low.
Trip no further, pretty sweeting;
Journeys end in lovers meeting,
  Every wise man's son does know.

Sir Andrew Extremely good indeed!

Sir Toby Good, good.

Feste *What is love? 'Tis not hereafter*
Present mirth has present laughter;
  What's to come is still unsure.
In delay there lies no plenty
Then come kiss me, sweet and twenty,
  Youth's a stuff will not endure.

Sir Andrew He has a mellifluous voice, as I'm a true knight. [*There are tears in his eyes*]

Sir Toby A very catchy bit of singing.

Sir Andrew Very sweet and catchy, indeed. [*He blows his nose emotionally*]

Sir Toby When you hear with your nose, that's catchiness at its sweetest. But shall we raise the roof? Shall we wake the night-owl by singing a catch that would draw three souls from a bible-punching weaver? Shall we do that?

Sir Andrew If you love me, let's do that! I'm dog at a catch! [*His slang for 'good'*]

Feste By heaven, sir, and some dogs are good at catching! [*He means retrievers*]

Sir Andrew   Most certain. Let our catch be, 'Thou knave'.

Feste   'Hold thy peace, thou knave', knight? I shall be
60   constrained in't to call thee knave, knight.

Sir Andrew   'Tis not the first time I have constrained one to
call me knave. Begin, fool; it begins 'Hold thy peace'.

Feste   I shall never begin if I hold my peace.

Sir Andrew   Good i' faith. Come, begin.

[They sing a catch]

[*Enter* **Maria**]

65   **Maria**   What a caterwauling do you keep here! If my lady
have not called up her steward Malvolio and bid him turn
you out of doors, never trust me.

Sir Toby   My lady's a Cataian; we are politicians; Malvolio's a
Peg-a-Ramsey, and 'Three merry men be we'. Am not I
70   consanguineous? Am I not of her blood? Tillyvally; lady!
[*Singing*] There dwelt a man in Babylon, lady, lady! –

Feste   Beshrew me, the knight's in admirable fooling.

Sir Andrew   Ay, he does well enough if he be disposed, and
so do I too; he does it with a better grace, but I do it more
75   natural.

Sir Toby   [*Singing*] O' the twelfth day of December –

Maria   For the love o' God, peace!

[*Enter* **Malvolio**]

Sir Andrew   [*missing the joke*] Very true. Let's choose as our
  catch 'You knave!'

Feste   'Hold your tongue, you knave'? That one, knight? I'll be
  forced to call you 'knave' in it, knight. [*This is because each
  singer passes a message round*]

Sir Andrew   It's not the first time I've forced someone to call
  me a knave. Begin, fool. It starts 'Hold your tongue'.

Feste   I'll never begin if I hold my tongue!

Sir Andrew   That's good, indeed! Come, on, let's begin.
  [*They sing the catch.* **Feste** *begins,* **Sir Toby** *follows, and* **Sir
  Andrew** *comes in last. There is a great deal of noise and
  merrymaking*]

  [**Maria** *enters*]

Maria   What a racket you're making! If my lady hasn't
  summoned her steward Malvolio and told him to turn you
  out of doors, never trust me again.

Sir Toby   My lady's got yellow skin, we're crafty, Malvolio's a
  prude and [*he bursts out into a loud chorus*] 'Three merry
  men be we!' Am I not a relation? Am I not of her blood?
  Rubbish! [*contemptuously*] My lady! [*cue for a song*] 'There
  dwelt a man in Babylon, lady, lady! –'

Feste   'Strewth – the knight's on top form!

Sir Andrew   Yes, he's good when he's in the mood, and so am
  I. He does it with more style, but I do it more naturally.

Sir Toby   [*really raucous now*] 'Oh, the twelfth day of
  December –'

Maria   For the love of God, keep it down!

  [**Malvolio** *enters*]

Malvolio   My masters, are you mad, or what are you? Have
you no wit, manners, nor honesty, but to gabble like tinkers
80   at this time of night? Do ye make an alehouse of my lady's
house, that ye squeak out your coziers' catches without any
mitigation or remorse of voice? Is there no respect of place,
persons, nor time in you?

Sir Toby   We did keep time, sir, in our catches. Sneck up!

85 **Malvolio**   Sir Toby, I must be round with you. My lady bade
me tell you that, though she harbours you as her kinsman,
she's nothing allied to your disorders. If you can separate
yourself and your misdemeanours, you are welcome to the
house; if not, an it would please you to take leave of her, she
90   is very willing to bid you farewell.

Sir Toby   [*Singing*] Farewell, dear heart, since I must needs be
gone.

Maria   Nay, good Sir Toby.

Feste   [*Singing*] His eyes do show his days are almost done.

95 **Malvolio**   Is't even so?

Sir Toby   [*Singing*] But I will never die.

Feste   [*Singing*] Sir Toby, there you lie.

Malvolio   This is much credit to you.

Sir Toby   [*Singing*] Shall I bid him go?

100 **Feste**   [*Singing*] What an if you do?

Sir Toby   [*Singing*] Shall I bid him go, and spare not?

Feste   [*Singing*] O! no, no, no, no, you dare not.

Malvolio   Gentlemen: are you mad, or what? Have you no
sense, manners or propriety to be gabbling like tinkers at
this time of night? Do you want to make an ale-house of my
lady's home, with your shoe-mender's songs squawked out
at the tops of your voices? Is there no respect in you for
where you are; or other people; or what time it is?

Sir Toby   We kept time, sir, in our catches! Belt up!

Malvolio   Sir Toby, I must be straight with you. My lady told
me to tell you that though she gives you a home here as one
of her kindred, she's no way related to your bad behaviour.
If you can part company with your misconduct, you are
welcome in the house. If you can't, and you'd like to go,
she's very willing to bid you farewell!

Sir Toby   [*still in a singing vein*] 'Farewell, dear heart, since I
must needs be gone –'

Maria   [*trying to restrain him*] Now then, good Sir Toby.

Feste   [*singing the second line of the song*] 'His eyes do show
his days are almost done –'

Malvolio   So that's it!

Sir Toby   [*oblivious: he goes on to line three*] 'But I will never
die!'

Feste   [*making up a fourth line*] 'Sir Toby, there you lie!'

Malvolio   Very creditable, I'm sure!

Sir Toby   [*conversing in song*] 'Shall I tell him to go?'

Feste   [*singing his reply*] 'What would happen if you did?'

Sir Toby   [*keeping to the tune*] 'Shall I tell him to go, and care
not?'

Feste   [*final line*] 'Oh, no, no, no, no! You dare not!'

Sir Toby   Out o' tune, sir! ye lie. Art any more than a
steward? Dost thou think, because thou art virtuous, there
105   shall be no more cakes and ale?

Feste   Yes, by Saint Anne; and ginger shall be hot i' the mouth
too.

Sir Toby   Thou'rt i' the right. Go, sir, rub your chain with
crumbs. A stoup of wine, Maria!

110 **Malvolio**   Mistress Mary, if you prized my lady's favour at
anything more than contempt, you would not give means
for this uncivil rule; she shall know of it, by this hand.

[*Exit*]

Maria   Go shake your ears.

Sir Andrew   'Twere as good a deed as to drink when a man's
115   a-hungry, to challenge him the field, and then to break
promise with him and make a fool of him.

Sir Toby   Do't, knight; I'll write thee a challenge; or I'll
deliver thy indignation to him by word of mouth.

Maria   Sweet Sir Toby, be patient for tonight; since the youth
120   of the count's was today with my lady, she is much out of
quiet. For Monsieur Malvolio, let me alone with him; if I do
not gull him into a nayword, and make him a common
recreation, do not think I have wit enough to lie straight in
my bed. I know I can do it.

125 **Sir Toby**   Possess us, possess us.

Sir Andrew   Tell us something of him.

Maria   Marry, sir, sometimes he is a kind of Puritan.

Sir Andrew   O! if I thought that, I'd beat him like a dog.

Sir Toby   What, for being a Puritan? Thy exquisite reason,
130   dear knight!

Sir Toby   That's out of tune, sir! That's a lie! [*To* **Malvolio**, *to show he's not afraid*] Are you any more than a *steward*? D'you think, because you're so virtuous, there'll be no more fun and games?

Feste   Yes, by St Anne! And ginger will still be hot stuff, too! (*Exit*)

Sir Toby   [*To* **Feste**] You're right. [*To* **Malvolio**] Go, sir: polish your chain! A flagon of wine, Maria!

Malvolio   Miss Mary, if you valued my lady's good opinion at anything more than contempt, you wouldn't supply the drink for this disorderly conduct. She shall hear of this, by this hand! [*He shakes it in the air and goes, angrily*]

Maria   Go and shake your ears! [*Like a donkey, she means*]

Sir Andrew   That's as good as giving a man a drink who's hungry, to provoke a duel, and then not turning up, to make a fool of him!

Sir Toby   Do that, knight! I'll write you a challenge: or I'll deliver your insult to him by word of mouth!

Maria   Sweet Sir Toby, be patient for tonight, Since the Count's young man visited my lady today, she's been very touchy. As for Mister Malvollo, leave him to me. If I don't trick him into being a byword for stupidity, and make him everybody's fool, don't credit me with the brains to lie straight in my bed. I know I can do it.

Sir Toby   Tell us how, tell us how!

Sir Andrew   Tell us something about him.

Maria   Well, sir, sometimes he is a kind of puritan.

Sir Andrew   Oh, if I thought that, I'd beat him like a dog!

Sir Toby   What, for being a puritan? Your subtle reason, dear knight?

Sir Andrew   I have no exquisite reason for 't, but I have
reason good enough.

Maria   The devil a Puritan that he is, or anything constantly,
but a time-pleaser, an affectioned ass, that cons state without
135   book, and utters it by great swarths; the best persuaded of
himself; so crammed, as he thinks, with excellences, that it is
his ground of faith that all that look on him love him; and on
that vice in him will my revenge find notable cause to work.

Sir Toby   What wilt thou do?

140   **Maria**   I will drop in his way some obscure epistles of love;
wherein, by the colour of his beard, the shape of his leg, the
manner of his gait, the expressure of his eye, forehead, and
complexion, he shall find himself most feelingly personated.
I can write very like my lady your niece; on a forgotten
145   matter we can hardly make distinction of our hands.

Sir Toby   Excellent! I smell a device.

Sir Andrew   I have 't in my nose, too.

Sir Toby   He shall think, by the letters that thou wilt drop,
that they come from my niece, and that she's in love with
150   him.

Maria   My purpose is, indeed, a horse of that colour.

Sir Andrew   And your horse now would make him an ass.

Maria   Ass, I doubt not.

Sir Andrew   O! 'twill be admirable.

155   **Maria**   Sport royal, I warrant you; I know my physic will work
with him. I will plant you two, and let the fool make a third,
where he shall find the letter; observe his construction of it.
For this night, to bed, and dream on the event. Farewell.

[Exit]

Sir Andrew   I haven't got a subtle reason, but I have a reason
that's good enough.

Maria   The devil a puritan he is, or anything consistently. He's
a time-server, an affected ass, that uses impressive phrases
without knowing their origin, uttering them by the yard. He's
got a very high opinion of himself. He's so crammed with
excellences, so he thinks, that it's his firm belief that all
who look on him, love him. And on that weakness of his, my
revenge will work itself out.

Sir Toby   What will you do?

Maria   I'll drop some love letters in his path, ambiguously
written. In them, he'll find himself closely described by the
colour of his beard, the shape of his legs, the way he walks,
the expression of his eye, his forehead and his complexion. I
can write very like your niece, my lady. Sometimes we can't
remember who wrote what.

Sir Toby   Excellent! I smell a rat! . . .

Sir Andrew   I can smell it, too!

Sir Toby   He'll think, by the letters you'll leave around, that
they come from my niece, and that she's in love with him!

Maria   I'm betting on a horse of that sort, yes.

Sir Andrew   And your horse will make him an ass!

Maria   Ass-suredly.

Sir Andrew   Oh, that will be admirable!

Maria   Sport royal, I guarantee you. I know my medicine will
do the trick. I'll plant you two, and let the fool make a third,
where he'll find the letter. Notice how he interprets it! For
tonight: to bed, and dream about the plan. Farewell!

[*She skips off*]

Sir Toby   Good night, Penthesilea.

160 **Sir Andrew**   Before me, she's a good wench.

Sir Toby   She's a beagle, true-bred, and one that adores me;
what o' that?

Sir Andrew   I was adored once too.

Sir Toby   Let's to bed, knight. Thou hadst need send for
165   more money.

Sir Andrew   If I cannot recover your niece, I am a foul way
out.

Sir Toby   Send for money, knight; if thou hast her not i' the
end, call me cut.

170 **Sir Andrew**   If I do not, never trust me, take it how you will.

Sir Toby   Come, come; I'll go burn some sack; 'tis too late to
go to bed now. Come, knight; come knight.

[*Exeunt*]

Scene 4

The Duke's Palace. Enter **Duke**, **Viola**, **Curio**, *and others*

Duke   Give me some music. Now, good morrow, friends.
Now, good Cesario, but that piece of song,
5   That old and antique song we heard last night;
Methought it did relieve my passion much,
More than light airs and recollected terms

Sir Toby   [*blowing her a kiss*] Goodnight, queen of the
Amazons!

Sir Andrew   Indeed, she's a good wench.

Sir Toby   She's a beagle, a thoroughbred, and one who adores
me. What do you think of that?

Sir Andrew   I was adored once, too.

Sir Toby   Let's go to bed, knight. You'd better send for more
money.

Sir Andrew   If I don't get your niece, I'm in a right mess.

Sir Toby   Send for money, knight. If you don't get her in the
end, call me horseface.

Sir Andrew   If I don't, never trust me again. You can take it
how you like.

Sir Toby   Come on, come on. I'll go and warm up some wine.
It's too late to go to bed now. Come on, knight. Come on,
knight.

[*They totter off, supporting each other*]

Scene 4

A room in the Duke's palace. Enter the **Duke, Viola, Curio** *and
others*

Duke   Let me hear some music. Now then: good morning,
friends. Now, good Cesario, just that little song, that old
and charming song, we heard last night. I thought it relieved
my feelings greatly, far more than the light airs and

Of these most brisk and giddy-paced times.
Come; but one verse.

10 **Curio**   He is not here, so please your lordship, that should
sing it.

Duke   Who was it?

Curio   Feste, the jester, my lord; a fool that the lady Olivia's
father took much delight in. He is about the house.

15 **Duke**   Seek him out, and play the tune the while.

[*Exit* **Curio**]

Come hither, boy: if ever thou shalt love,
In the sweet pangs of it remember me;
For such as I am all true lovers are,
Unstaid and skittish in all motions else
20 Save in the constant image of the creature
That is beloved. How dost thou like this tune?

Viola   It gives a very echo to the seat
Where Love is throned.

Duke   Thou dost speak masterly.
My life upon 't, young though thou art, thine eye
25 Hath stayed upon some favour that it loves;
Hath it not, boy?

Viola   A little, by your favour.

Duke   What kind of woman is't?

Viola   Of your complexion.

Duke   She is not worth thee, then. What years, i'faith?

Viola   About your years, my lord.

30 **Duke**   Too old, by heaven. Let still the woman take
An elder than herself, so wears she to him,

ingenious melodies of our fast and dizzy-making times.
Come: just one verse.

Curio   The man who sings it isn't here, so please your
lordship.

Duke   Who was it?

Curio   Feste, the jester, my lord: a fool much appreciated by
the lady Olivia's father. He's around the house.

Duke   Find him, and meanwhile play the tune.

[**Curio** *goes. The music plays*]

[*To* **Viola**] Come here, boy. If you ever fall in love, in the
sweet agony of it remember me. Because as I am now, so
are all true lovers: unstable and fickle in everything except in
their obsession with the creature that is loved. How do you
like this tune?

Viola   It echoes precisely the centre of love's being.

Duke   You speak like an expert! Upon my life, young though
you are, you have your eye on someone you love. Isn't that
so, boy?

Viola   Just a little, if I may say so to you.

Duke   What kind of woman is she?

Viola   She looks like you.

Duke   She's not worthy of you then! How old, indeed?

Viola   About your age, my lord.

Duke   Too old, by heaven! The woman should always marry
someone older than herself, so that she adjusts to suit him,

So sways she level in her husband's heart;
For, boy, however we do praise ourselves,
Our fancies are more giddy and unfirm,
35   More longing, wavering, sooner lost and worn,
Than women's are.

Viola   I think it well, my lord.

Duke   Then let thy love be younger than thyself,
Or thy affection cannot hold the bent;
For women are as roses, whose fair flower
40   Being once displayed, doth fall that very hour.

Viola   And so they are; alas, that they are so!
To die, even when they to perfection grow.

[*Enter* **Curio** *and* **Feste**]

Duke   O, fellow! come, the song we had last night.
Mark it, Cesario; it is old and plain;
45   The spinsters and the knitters in the sun,
And the free maids that weave their thread with bones,
Do use to chant it; it is silly sooth,
And dallies with the innocence of love,
Like the old age.

50   **Feste**   Are you ready, sir?

Duke   Ay; prithee sing.

Feste   [*Singing*]   *Come away, come away, death,*
                    And in sad cypress let me be laid;
                    Fly away, fly away, breath;
55   *I am slain by a fair cruel maid.*
                    My shroud of white, stuck all with yew,
                       O! prepare it;
                    My part of death, no one so true
                       Did share it.

and so that she keeps a steady place in her husband's heart. Because, boy, no matter how we flatter ourselves, our inclinations are more giddy and fickle, more desirous and inconstant, more easily spent and exhausted, than women's are.

Viola   I think that's right, my lord.

Duke   So see that your love is younger than you are, or your love can't last. Women are like roses, whose blooms begin to fall within the hour they're first displayed.

Viola   And so they are. Alas that they're like that, to die just when they've reached perfection!

[**Curio** *returns with* **Feste**]

Duke   Oh, fellow! Come, let's have the song we had last night. Take note of it, Cesario: it's old and plain. Spinning-women and knitters in the sunshine, unmarried maids who make lace with thread and shuttles, they often sing it. It is simple truthfulness, and its subject is the innocence of love, as it was in days gone by.

Feste   Are you ready sir?

Duke   Yes. Please: sing.

[*The music begins*]

Feste   [*singing*]   *Come away, come away death,*
                    And in sad cypress let me be laid;
                 Fly away, fly away breath,
                    I am slain by a fair, cruel maid.
                 My shroud of white, stuck all with yew
                       O! prepare it;
                 My part of death, no one so true
                       Did share it.

93

60   *Not a flower, not a flower sweet,*
            On my black coffin let there be strown;
        Not a friend, not a friend greet
            My poor corpse, where my bones shall be
                thrown;
65   *A thousand thousand sighs to save,*
            Lay me O! where
        Sad true lover never find my grave,
            To weep there.

Duke   There's for thy pains.

70 **Feste**   No pains, sir; I take pleasure in singing, sir.

Duke   I'll pay thy pleasure, then.

Feste   Truly, sir, and pleasure will be paid, one time or another.

Duke   Give me now leave to leave thee.

75 **Feste**   Now, the melancholy god protect thee, and the tailor make thy doublet of changeable taffeta, for thy mind is a very opal! I would have men of such constancy put to sea, that their business might be everything and their intent everywhere; for that's it that always makes a good voyage of
80   nothing. Farewell.

                                                    [*Exit*]

Duke   Let all the rest give place.

                            [*Exeunt* **Curio** *and* **Attendants**]

                            Once more, Cesario,
        Get thee to yond same sovereign cruelty;
        Tell her, my love, more noble than the world,
        Prizes not quantity of dirty lands;
85   The parts that fortune hath bestowed upon her,

Not a flower, not a flower sweet
   On my black coffin let there be strown;
Not a friend, not a friend greet
   My poor corpse, where my bones shall be
      thrown;
A thousand thousand sighs to save
      Lay me O! where
Sad true lover never find my grave
      To weep there.

Duke   [*offering money*] That's for your trouble.

Feste   No trouble, sir. I take pleasure in singing, sir.

Duke   I'll pay your pleasure, then.

Feste   True sir: pleasure must be paid for sometime or other.

Duke   That's enough of that!

Feste   May the god of melancholy protect you, and your tailor
make your clothes of shot silk: because your mind has the
qualities of opal, that changes colour according to the light!
I'd have men with that kind of changeability put to sea.
Then their business would be everything and their
destinations everywhere. That's how an interesting voyage
can be made, through having no destination.

[*He goes*]

Duke   Everyone else can go.

[**Curio** *and the* **Attendants** *leave*]

Once more, Cesario, go to that ultimate in cruelty. Tell her
that my love, more noble than the world, puts no value on
large estates of sordid land. What good fortune has given

95

Tell her, I hold as giddily as fortune;
But 'tis that miracle and queen of gems
That nature pranks her in, attracts my soul.

Viola   But if she cannot love you, sir?

90 **Duke**   I cannot be so answered.

Viola   Sooth, but you must.
Say that some lady, as perhaps there is,
Hath for your love as great a pang of heart
As you have for Olivia; you cannot love her;
95   You tell her so; must she not then be answered?

Duke   There is no woman's sides
Can bide the beating of so strong a passion
As love doth give my heart; no woman's heart
So big, to hold so much; they lack retention.
100   Alas! their love may be called appetite,
No motion of the liver, but the palate,
That suffer surfeit, cloyment, and revolt;
But mine is all as hungry as the sea,
And can digest as much. Make no compare
105   Between that love a woman can bear me
And that I owe Olivia.

Viola   Ay, but I know –

Duke   What dost thou know?

Viola   Too well what love women to men may owe;
In faith, they are as true of heart as we.
110   My father had a daughter loved a man,
As it might be, perhaps, were I a woman,
I should your lordship.

Duke   And what's her history?

Viola . A blank, my lord. She never told her love,
But let concealment, like a worm i' the bud,

her, tell her I regard as the luck of the draw. What attracts my soul is her beauty, in which she's a miracle, a queen of gems.

Viola   What if she cannot love you, sir?

Duke   I can't accept that answer.

Viola   Truly, but you must. Suppose there were some lady – as perhaps there is – who has as painful a love for you as you have for Olivia. You cannot love her. You tell her so. Mustn't she accept that answer?

Duke   No woman's frame could stand the throbbing of so strong a passion as love gives to my heart. No woman's heart is so big, to cope with so much. Women lack staying power. Alas, their love could be called appetite. It's not the genuine article. It's something akin to taste: they can have too much; overeat; and feel revulsion. My appetite is as hungry as the sea's, and it can digest as much. Don't compare the love that a woman can have for me with how I feel about Olivia!

Viola   Yes, but I know   [*she stops, realizing she mustn't say too much*]

Duke   What do you know?

Viola   – only too well how women may love men. Indeed, they are as faithful as we are. My father had a daughter who loved a man; just as, perhaps, if I were a woman, I might love your lordship.

Duke   And what's her story?

Viola   A blank, my lord. She never revealed her love, but let her secret destroy the roses in her cheeks, like a worm

¹¹⁵   Feed on her damask cheek; she pined in thought,
        And with a green and yellow melancholy,
        She sat like Patience on a monument,
        Smiling at grief. Was not this love indeed?
        We men may say more, swear more; but indeed
¹²⁰   Our shows are more than will, for still we prove
        Much in our vows, but little in our love.

Duke   But died thy sister of her love, my boy?

Viola   I am all the daughters of my father's house,
        And all the brothers too; and yet I know not.
        Sir, shall I to this lady?

¹²⁵ **Duke**   Ay, that's the theme.
        To her in haste; give her this jewel; say
        My love can give no place, bide no denay.

                                          [*Exeunt*]

Scene 5

Olivia's Garden. Enter **Sir Toby Belch, Sir Andrew
Aguecheek,** *and* **Fabian**

Sir Toby   Come thy ways, Signior Fabian.

Fabian   Nay, I'll come; if I lose a scruple of this sport, let me
     be boiled to death with melancholy.

Sir Toby   Would'st thou not be glad to have the niggardly,
⁵   rascally sheep-biter come by some notable shame?

Fabian   I would exult, man; you know he brought me out o'
     favour with my lady about a bear-baiting here.

inside a bud. She pined in her thoughts, and sick in mind and body with her melancholy, she sat around like the figure of Patience on a monument, smiling at her grief. Wasn't this true love? We men may say more and swear more, but indeed our behaviour is insincere. We tend to vow a lot, but love little.

Duke   Did your sister die of her love, my boy?

Viola   [*with clever ambiguity*] I am all the daughters that my father has – and all the brothers, too, though I may be wrong. Sir, shall I go to this lady?

Duke   Yes, that's the idea. Go to her quickly. Give her this jewel. Say my love cannot yield, nor bear a denial.

Scene 5

Olivia's garden. Enter **Sir Toby Belch, Sir Andrew Aguecheek** *and* **Fabian**

Sir Toby   Come along, Mister Fabian!

Fabian   I'll come all right: if I miss a second of this game, may I be boiled to death with misery!

Sir Toby   Wouldn't you be delighted to have that mean, rascally back-biting dog thoroughly shamed?

Fabian   I would rejoice, man! You know he got me into trouble with my lady over bear-baiting here?

Sir Toby   To anger him we'll have the bear again, and we
will fool him black and blue; shall we not, Sir Andrew?

10 **Sir Andrew**   An we do not, it is pity of our lives.

[*Enter* **Maria**]

Sir Toby   Here comes the little villain. How now, my metal
of India?

Maria   Get ye all three into the box-tree. Malvolio's coming
down this walk; he has been yonder i' the sun, practising
15   behaviour to his own shadow this half hour. Observe him,
for the love of mockery; for I know this letter will make a
contemplative idiot of him. Close, in the name of jesting! Lie
thou there; [*She throws down a letter*] for here comes the trout
that must be caught with tickling.

[*Exit*]

[*Enter* **Malvolio**]

20 **Malvolio**   'Tis but fortune; all is fortune. Maria once told me
she did affect me; and I have heard herself come thus near,
that, should she fancy, it should be one of my complexion.
Besides, she uses me with a more exalted respect than any
one else that follows her. What should I think on't?

25 **Sir Toby**   Here's an overweening rogue!

Fabian   O, peace! Contemplation makes a rare turkey-cock of
him; how he jets under his advanced plumes!

Sir Andrew   'Slight, I could so beat the rogue!

Sir Toby   To make him angry we'll have bear-baiting here again, and we'll fool him something rotten. Shall we not, Sir Andrew?

Sir Andrew   If we don't, we'll regret it all our lives!

[**Maria** *enters*]

Sir Toby   Here comes the little villain. How's things, my precious one?

Maria   All three of you: hide behind the hedge. [*They do so*] Malvolio's coming down the path. He's been over there in the sun, practising bowing to his own shadow for the last half hour. Watch him, for the love of mockery – because I know this letter [*she produces one from her bosom*] will make a blithering idiot of him. Keep down, in the name of practical joking! [*She throws the letter down on the path*] Lie there, for here comes a trout who'll be caught by tickling!

[*She goes*]

[**Malvolio** *enters, talking to himself*]

Malvolio   It's all a matter of luck; everything is a matter of luck. Maria once told me she fancied me, and I've heard her hint that if she ever fell for anyone, it would be my type. Besides, she treats me with greater respect than anyone else who pursues her. What should I make of that?

Sir Toby   [*to* **Sir Andrew** *and* **Fabian**, *whispering*] Here's a conceited rogue!

Fabian   Sh! Reverie makes a rare peacock of him. How he displays himself beneath his raised plumes!

Sir Andrew   'Strewth, I really could beat the rogue!

101

30 **Sir Toby**   Peace! I say!

Malvolio   To be Count Malvolio!

Sir Toby   Ah, rogue!

Sir Andrew   Pistol him, pistol him.

Sir Toby   Peace! peace!

Malvolio   There is example for 't; the lady of the Strachy
35   married the yeoman of the wardrobe.

Sir Andrew   Fie on him, Jezebel!

Fabian   O, peace! now he's deeply in; look how imagination
blows him.

Malvolio   Having been three months married to her, sitting
40   in my state, –

Sir Toby   O! for a stone-bow, to hit him in the eye.

Malvolio   Calling my officers about me, in my branched
velvet gown; having come from a day-bed, where I have left
Olivia sleeping, –

45 **Sir Toby**   Fire and brimstone!

Fabian   O, peace! peace!

Malvolio   And then to have the humour of state; and after a
demure travel of regard, telling them I know my place, as I
would they should do theirs, to ask for my kinsman Toby, –

50 **Sir Toby**   Bolts and shackles!

Fabian   O, peace, peace, peace! Now, now.

Malvolio   Seven of my people, with an obedient start, make
out for him. I frown the while, and perchance wind up my

Sir Toby   Quiet, will you?

Malvolio   To be Count Malvolio!

Sir Toby   [*unable to hold it in*] Ah, you rogue!

Sir Andrew   Shoot him, shoot him!

Sir Toby   Quiet, quiet!

Malvolio   There's a precedent for it. That Strachy lady married
her head wardrobe man.

Sir Andrew   Curse him, Jezebel!

Fabian   Oh, quiet! He's far gone. Look how he swells with his
thoughts!

Malvolio   Having been married to her for three months, sitting
in my chair of state –

Sir Toby   If only I had a catapult to hit him in the eye!

Malvolio   – calling my servants to me, dressed in my ornate
velvet gown, having come from a day-bed, where I have left
Olivia sleeping –

Sir Toby   Fire and brimstone!

Fabian   [*holding him down*] Oh quiet, quiet!

Malvolio   I'd then be in the mood for some business; and after
viewing them all solemnly, telling them that I know my place
as I would want them to know theirs, I'd ask for my kinsman
Toby –

Sir Toby   Bolts and shackles!

Fabian   [*doing his best to restrain him*] Oh, quiet, quiet, quiet!
Now, now . . .

Malvolio   Seven of my people, jerking to attention obediently,
go looking for him. I frown meanwhile, and perhaps wind up

55   watch, or play with my – some rich jewel. Toby approaches,
      curtsies there to me, –

Sir Toby   Shall this fellow live?

Fabian   Though our silence be drawn from us with cars, yet
      peace!

Malvolio   I extend my hand to him thus, quenching my
60   familiar smile with an austere regard of control, –

Sir Toby   And does not Toby take you a blow o' the lips
      then?

Malvolio   Saying, 'Cousin Toby, my fortunes, having cast me
      on your niece, give me this prerogative of speech,' –

65 **Sir Toby**   What, what?

Malvolio   'You must amend your drunkenness.'

Sir Toby   Out, scab!

Fabian   Nay, patience, or we break the sinews of our plot.

Malvolio   'Besides, you waste the treasure of your time with a
70   foolish knight,' –

Sir Andrew   That's me, I warrant you.

Malvolio   'One Sir Andrew,' –

Sir Andrew   I knew't was I; for many do call me fool.

Malvolio   [*Seeing the letter*] What employment have we here?

75 **Fabian**   Now is the woodcock near the gin.

Sir Toby   O, peace! and the spirit of humours intimate
      reading aloud to him!

my watch, or play with my [*he touches his steward's chain
forgetfully, then remembers he wouldn't be wearing
one*] – some rich jewel. Toby approaches; bows to me –

Sir Toby   [*apoplectic now*] Shall this fellow be allowed to live?

Fabian   Even if wild horses tried to drag words out of
us – *quiet*!

Malvolio   I extend my hand to him like this [*he demonstrates
by stretching one out limply and condescendingly*],
suppressing my smile of familiarity beneath an austere look
of authority –

Sir Toby   And doesn't Toby hit you in the mouth, then?

Malvolio   – saying 'Cousin Toby. Good fortune having won me
your niece, I have the right to say this –'

Sir Toby   What, what?

Malvolio   'You must remedy your drunkenness.'

Sir Toby   Away, you scab!

Fabian   No – do be patient, or we'll give the game away.

Malvolio   – 'Besides, you waste your precious time with a
foolish knight' –

Sir Andrew   That's me, you know.

Malvolio   – 'one Sir Andrew' –

Sir Andrew   I knew it was me. Lots of people call me a fool.

Malvolio   [*spotting the letter on the ground*] Now what can
this be?

Fabian   Now our bird is near the trap . . .

Sir Toby   Sh! May he be inspired to read it aloud!

Malvolio   By my life, this is my lady's hand! These be her
very C's, her U's and her T's; and thus makes she her great
80   P's. It is, in contempt of question, her hand.

Sir Andrew   Her C's, her U's and her T's; why that?

Malvolio   [*Reading*] To the unknown beloved, this, and my
good wishes; Her very phrases! By your leave, wax. [*He opens
the letter*] Soft! and the impressure her Lucrece, with which
85   she uses to seal; 'tis my lady. To whom should this be?

Fabian   This wins him, liver and all.

Malvolio   [*Reading*]   Jove knows I love;
                                          But who?
                                          Lips, do not move:
90   No man must know.

'No man must know.' What follows? The number's altered!
'No man must know.' If this should be thee, Malvolio?

Sir Toby   Marry, hang thee, brock!

Malvolio   [*Reading*]   I may command where I adore;
95   But silence, like a Lucrece knife,
                                              With bloodless stroke my heart doth
                                                  gore:
                                              M, O, A, I, doth sway my life.

Fabian   A fustian riddle!

100 **Sir Toby**   Excellent wench, say I.

Malvolio   'M, O, A, I, doth sway my life.' Nay, but first, let
me see, let me see, let me see.

Malvolio   [*Picking up the letter*] By my life, this is my lady's handwriting! This is how she does her C's, her U's and her T's. That's how she writes her capital P's. It is, beyond a doubt, her handwriting.

Sir Andrew   Her C's, her U's and her T's? What does he mean?

Malvolio   [*Reading*] *To the unknown beloved: this letter and my good wishes.* Her very style! [*He decides to open it*] With your permission, wax! [*He breaks the wax seal*] Well, it's even stamped with her personal seal with Lucretia on it, which she always uses on letters. It's from my lady all right. To whom has it been sent?

Fabian   This will convince him, heart and soul!

Malvolio   [*Reading the letter's contents*]

> *God knows I love;*
>   *But who?*
> *Lips, do not move:*
> *No man must know.*

'No man must know'? What's after that? The metre changes. 'No man must know'. What if it should be you, Malvolio?

Sir Toby   May you be hanged, braggart!

Malvolio   [*Reading*]

> *I may command where I adore*
> *But silence, like Lucretia's knife*
> *With bloodless stroke my heart does gore*
> *M, O, A, I, does sway my life.*

Fabian   A fatuous riddle!

Sir Toby   Excellent woman, say I!

Malvolio   'M, O, A, I, does sway my life.' [*He thinks*] Yes, but first, let me see, let me see, let me see . . .

Fabian   What a dish o' poison has she dressed him!

Sir Toby   And with what wing the staniel checks at it!

105 **Malvolio**   'I may command where I adore.' Why, she may command me; I serve her: she is my lady. Why, this is evident to any formal capacity; and there is no obstruction in this. And the end, – What should that alphabetical position portend? If I could make that resemble something in
110 me – softly! *M, O, A, I,* –

Sir Toby   O! ay, make up that; he is now at a cold scent.

Fabian   Sowter will cry upon't, for all this, though it be as rank as a fox.

Malvolio   *M,* Malvolio; *M,* why, that begins my name!

115 **Fabian**   Did not I say he would work it out? The cur is excellent at faults.

Malvolio   *M,* – but then there is no consonancy in the sequel; that suffers under probation; *A* should follow, but *O* does.

Fabian   And *O* shall end, I hope.

120 **Sir Toby**   Ay, or I'll cudgel him, and make him cry *O!*

Malvolio   And then *I* comes behind.

Fabian   Ay, an you had any eye behind you, you might see more detraction at your heels than fortunes before you.

Malvolio   *M, O, A, I;* this simulation is not as the former; and
125 yet, to crush this a little, it would bow to me, for every one of these letters are in my name. Soft! here follows prose. [*Reading*] 'If this fall into thy hand, revolve! In my stars I am

Fabian   What a dish of poison she's prepared for him!

Sir Toby   And how quickly the hawk takes the bait!

Malvolio   'I may command where I adore.' Why, she may command me! I serve her. She is my lady. Why, this is obvious to anyone with normal brains. There's no problem here. And the end – what does that arrangement of letters signify? If I could make that relate to something in me. [*He thinks hard*] Wait a moment! [*He thinks he has got it*] M, O, A, I, –

Sir Toby   [*mimicking the sounds of two of these letters*] Oh, ay: follow that . . . now he's gone cold.

Fabian   In spite of that, Bonzo will pick up the scent again, though it's been stinking like a fox all the time!

Malvolio   M, Malvolio; M – why that begins my name!

Fabian   Didn't I say he would work it out? The dog is excellent at dropping and picking up scents.

Malvolio   M . . . But then there is no system in the sequel. It doesn't hold together. A should follow, but O does.

Fabian   And O shall end it, I hope. [*meaning 'woe'*]

Sir Toby   Yes, or I'll beat him and make him cry O! [*meaning 'Oh!'*]

Malvolio   And then I comes at the end.

Fabian   Yes, and if you had an 'eye' behind you, you might see more scorn to your rear than good fortune ahead!

Malvolio   M, O, A, I; this problem is not like the first one [*he means the words on the outside of the letter*], and yet if I force it a little it will fit me: for each of these letters is in my name. Ah, here follows prose: [*He reads*] *'If this falls into your hands, consider! By the chance of fortune, I am above*

above thee; but be not afraid of greatness; some are born
great, some achieve greatness, and some have greatness
130   thrust upon them. Thy Fates open their hands; let thy blood
and spirit embrace them, and to inure thyself to what thou
art like to be, cast thy humble slough and appear fresh. Be
opposite with a kinsman, surly with servants; let thy tongue
tang arguments of state; put thyself into the trick of
135   singularity: she thus advises thee that sighs for thee.
Remember who commended thy yellow stockings, and
wished to see thee ever cross-gartered; I say, remember. Go
to, thou art made if thou desirest to be so; if not, let me see
thee a steward still, the fellow of servants, and not worthy to
140   touch Fortune's fingers. Farewell. She that would alter
services with thee,

                       The Fortunate-Unhappy'

Daylight and champain discovers not more. This is open. I
will be proud, I will read politic authors, I will baffle Sir
Toby, I will wash off gross acquaintance, I will be point-
145   devise the very man. I do not now fool myself, to let
imagination jade me; for every reason excites to this, that my
lady loves me. She did commend my yellow stockings of late;
she did praise my leg being cross-gartered; and in this she
manifests herself to my love, and with a kind of injunction
150   drives me to these habits of her liking. I thank my stars I am
happy. I will be strange, stout, in yellow stockings, and
cross-gartered, even with the swiftness of putting on. Jove
and my stars be praised! Here is yet a postscript.

[*Reading*] 'Thou canst not choose but know who I am. If thou
155   entertainest my love, let it appear in thy smiling; thy smile
becomes thee well; therefore in my presence still smile, dear
my sweet, I prithee.'

Jove, I thank thee. I will smile; I will do everything that thou
wilt have me.

                                           [*Exit*]

*you, but don't be afraid of greatness: some are born great,
some achieve greatness, and some have greatness thrust
upon them. The Fates offer their helping hands; let your
courage and spirits grasp them; and to prepare yourself for
what you are likely to be, cast off your humble exterior, and
take on a new look. Be argumentative with a certain
kinsman; surly with servants; let your speech be about lofty
matters; be an individualist. She who sighs for you gives you
this advice. Remember who praised your yellow stockings,
and wished to see you cross-gartered. I say again:
remember. Right, then: you are made if you want to be; if
not, stay a steward forever, with servants as your fellows,
not worthy to touch Fortune's fingers. Farewell. She who
would change ranks with you,*

> *The Fortunate-Unhappy.'*

It's as plain as daylight and open country! This is perfectly
plain. I *shall* be proud; I *shall* read weighty authors; I *shall*
clash with Sir Toby; I *shall* cut my common friends. Down to
the last detail, I'll be the very man. I'm not fooling myself,
letting my imagination make an ass of me. Everything
points to this: that my lady loves me. She *did* praise my
yellow stockings recently; she *did* praise my legs being
cross-gartered. In this [*he waves the letter*] she clearly
shows that she loves me, and with heavy hints guides me
towards these practices, which she likes. I thank my lucky
stars that I'm fortunate. I will be distant, haughty, in yellow
stockings, *and* cross-gartered, as fast as I can put them on.
May Jove and my stars be praised! [*He turns the letter over*]
There's a postscript, too:

[*Reading*] *'You cannot help but know who I am. If you
reciprocate my love, show it in your smiling. You have a lovely
smile. So in my presence, always smile, my dear
sweetheart, I beg you.'*

I thank you, Jove. I *shall* smile. [*He practises: the effect is
rather gruesome*] I'll do everything you want me to.

> [*He leaves, smiling his awful smile*]

160 **Fabian**   I will not give my part of this sport for a pension of
thousands to be paid from the Sophy.

Sir Toby   I could marry this wench for this device.

Sir Andrew   So could I too.

Sir Toby   And ask no other dowry with her but such another
165   jest.

Sir Andrew   Nor I neither.

Fabian   Here comes my noble gull-catcher.

[*Enter* **Maria**]

Sir Toby   Wilt thou set thy foot o' my neck?

Sir Andrew   Or o' mine either?

170 **Sir Toby**   Shall I play my freedom at tray-trip, and become
thy bondslave?

Sir Andrew   I' faith, or I either?

Sir Toby   Why, thou hast put him in such a dream, that
when the image of it leaves him he must run mad.

175 **Maria**   Nay, but say true; does it work upon him?

Sir Toby   Like aqua-vitae with a midwife.

Maria   If you will then see the fruits of the sport, mark his
first approach before my lady; he will come to her in yellow
stockings, and 'tis a colour she abhors; and cross-gartered, a
180   fashion she detests; and he will smile upon her, which will
now be so unsuitable to her disposition, being addicted to a
melancholy as she is, that it cannot but turn him into a
notable contempt. If you will see it, follow me.

Sir Toby   To the gates of Tartar, thou most excellent devil of
185   wit.

112

Fabian   I wouldn't give away my share in this joke for a
pension of thousands to be paid by the Shah of Persia!

Sir Toby   I could marry the girl for this hoax.

Sir Andrew   I could, too.

Sir Toby   And ask for no other dowry with her but another
joke like this!

Sir Andrew   Me too.

Fabian   Here comes our noble hoaxer!

[**Maria** *returns*]

Sir Toby   Shall I gamble at cards with you, my freedom as the
stake, and become your slave?

Sir Andrew   Indeed, or shall I?

Sir Toby   Why, you've put him in such a dream that when he
comes out of it he'll go mad, for sure!

Maria   No, tell the truth; do you think it worked?

Sir Toby   Like brandy with a midwife!

Maria   If you want to see the joke come to fruition, observe
his first approach to my lady. He will come to her in yellow
stockings, which is a colour she loathes. And cross-gartered, a
fashion she detests. And he will smile at her,
which will be so inappropriate to her mood, being inclined to
sadness as she is, that it must make him very
objectionable. If you want to see it, follow me!

Sir Toby   To the gates of hell, you most excellent devil of jest!

Sir Andrew I'll make one too.

[*Exeunt*]

Sir Andrew   I'll go with you.

[*They leave, laughing*]

Act three

Scene 1

Olivia's Garden. Enter **Viola** *and* **Feste** *with a tabor*

Viola Save thee, friend, and thy music! Dost thou live by thy tabor?

Feste No, sir, I live by the church.

Viola Art thou a churchman?

5 **Feste** No such matter, sir; I do live by the church, for I do live at my house, and my house doth stand by the church.

Viola So thou mayest say, the king lies by a beggar if a beggar dwell near him; or, the church stands by thy tabor, if thy tabor stand by the church.

10 **Feste** You have said, sir. To see this age! A sentence is but a cheveril glove to a good wit; how quickly the wrong side may be turned outward!

Viola Nay, that's certain; they that dally nicely with words may quickly make them wanton.

15 **Feste** I would therefore my sister had had no name, sir.

Viola Why, man?

Feste Why, sir, her name's a word; and to dally with that word might make my sister wanton. But indeed words are very rascals since bonds disgraced them.

20 **Viola** Thy reason, man?

Act three

Scene 1

Olivia's garden. Enter **Viola** *and* **Feste**, *who is carrying a small drum.*

Viola   Greetings, friend, and your music too. Do you live by drumming?

Feste   No, sir. I live by the church.

Viola   Are you a cleric?

Feste   Not at all, sir. I live by the church because I live at my house, and my house is near the church.

Viola   So you could just as well say 'The King lives by begging' if a beggar lives near him. Or that the church is near your drum if the drum happens to be near the church.

Feste   You've said it, sir! Such are the times! A sentence is just a kid glove to a quick-witted man. It can easily be turned inside out!

Viola   Yes, that's true. Those who play about with words can quickly give them indecent meanings.

Feste   Therefore I wish my sister had no name, sir.

Viola   Why, man?

Feste   Why, sir, her name is a word, and to play about with that word might make my sister indecent. But indeed, words have become little rascals since they were disgraced with being bonds. [*He's referring to the expression 'my word is my bond'*]

Viola   Your reason, man?

117

Feste   Troth, sir, I can yield you none without words; and
words are grown so false, I am loath to prove reason with
them.

Viola   I warrant thou art a merry fellow, and carest for
25   nothing.

Feste   Not so, sir; I do care for something; but in my
conscience, sir, I do not care for you; if that be to care for
nothing, sir, I would it would make you invisible.

Viola   Art not thou the Lady Olivia's fool?

30 **Feste**   No, indeed, sir; the Lady Olivia has no folly; she will
keep no fool, sir, till she be married; and fools are as like
husbands as pilchards are to herrings – the husband's the
bigger. I am indeed not her fool, but her corrupter of words.

Viola   I saw thee late at the Count Orsino's.

35 **Feste**   Foolery, sir, does walk about the orb like the sun: it
shines everywhere. I would be sorry, sir, but the fool should
be as oft with your master as with my mistress. I think I saw
your wisdom there.

Viola   Nay, an thou pass upon me, I'll no more with thee.
40   Hold, there's expenses for thee.

Feste   Now Jove, in his next commodity of hair, send thee a
beard!

Viola   By my troth, I'll tell thee, I am almost sick for one,
though I would not have it grow on my chin. Is thy lady
45   within?

Feste   Would not a pair of these have bred, sir?

Viola   Yes, being kept together and put to use.

Feste 'Strewth, sir, I can't give you one without using words, and words have become so unreliable, I'm reluctant to use them to prove a reason.

Viola You're a happy-go-lucky fellow, I'll be bound, and you care about nothing.

Feste Not at all, sir. I do care for something. But upon my conscience, sir, I don't care for you. If that's caring about nothing, sir, I wish it would make you invisible.

Viola Aren't you the Lady Olivia's fool?

Feste No indeed, sir. Lady Olivia does not go in for entertainment. She won't have a fool till she's married: and fools are as like husbands as pilchards are to herrings – the husband's the bigger. Indeed I am not her fool. I'm her corrupter of words.

Viola I saw you recently at Count Orsino's.

Feste Foolery, sir, orbits like the sun: it shines everywhere. I'd be sorry, sir, if the fool were not as often with your master as my mistress. Didn't I see your wise self there?

Viola Well now, if you make fun of me, I'll stay with you no longer. Hold on. [**Viola** *searches her purse*] There's something for you to spend. [*She gives him some money*]

Feste [*mocking* **Viola**'*s smooth skin*] May God send you a beard when he has more in stock!

Viola Upon my word, I can tell you I'm almost sick for one [*she means Orsino's*] but I wouldn't have it grow on *my* chin! Is your lady at home?

Feste [*looking at his tip*] Wouldn't a pair of these breed more, sir?

Viola Yes, kept together and put to use.

Feste   I would play Lord Pandarus of Phrygia, sir, to bring a
Cressida to this Troilus.

50 **Viola**   I understand you, sir; 'tis well begged.

Feste   The matter, I hope, is not great, sir, begging but a
beggar; Cressida was a beggar. My lady is within, sir. I will
construe to them whence you come; who you are and what
you would are out of my welkin; I might say 'element', but
55 the word is overworn.

[*Exit*]

Viola   This fellow's wise enough to play the fool,
And to do that well craves a kind of wit;
He must observe their mood on whom he jests,
The quality of persons, and the time,
60 Not, like the haggard, check at every feather
That comes before his eye. This is a practice
As full of labour as a wise man's art,
For folly that he wisely shows is fit;
But wise men, folly-fall'n, quite taint their wit.

[*Enter* **Sir Toby Belch** *and* **Sir Andrew Aguecheek**]

65 **Sir Toby**   Save you, gentleman.

Viola   And you, sir.

Sir Andrew   Dieu vous garde, monsieur.

Viola   Et vous aussi; votre serviteur.

Feste   I'd like to be a Pandarus and bring a Cressida to this
Troilus [*he holds up his coin*]. [*He's referring to the ancient
story of how the lovers Troilus and Cressida were aided by
their uncle Pandarus to sleep together*]

Viola   I understand you, sir. [*She offers an extra coin*] You've
begged it well.

Feste   Begging for a beggar is not wrong, I hope, Sir. –
Cressida was a beggar. My lady *is* at home, sir. I'll explain to
my lady and her servants where you've come from. Who you
are, and what you want, are beyond my short. I could say
'brief', but the word is overused.

[*He goes*]

Viola   This fellow is wise enough to be a professional fool, and
to do that well requires a kind of cleverness. He must assess
the moods of those he jokes about, their rank, and the
occasion. He can't behave like an untrained hawk,
snatching at every piece of bait that comes his way. This is
a job requiring as much hard work as the profession of a
wise man. His fooling, when it's intelligently done, is fit and
proper. But when wise men stoop to folly, they ruin their
reputations.

[*Enter* **Sir Toby Belch** *and* **Sir Andrew Aguecheek**]

Sir Toby   God be with you, gentleman.

Viola   And you, sir.

Sir Andrew   [*repeating* **Sir Toby**, *and showing off his French*]
Dieu vous guarde, monsieur.

Viola   [*responding fluently*] Et vous, aussi; votre serviteur.
[*And you too; your servant*]

121

Sir Andrew   I hope, sir, you are; and I am yours.

70 **Sir Toby**   Will you encounter the house? My niece is desirous
you should enter, if your trade be to her.

Viola   I am bound to your niece, sir; I mean, she is the list of
my voyage.

Sir Toby   Taste your legs, sir; put them to motion.

75 **Viola**   My legs do better under-stand me, sir, than I
understand what you mean by bidding me taste my legs.

Sir Toby   I mean, to go, sir, to enter.

Viola   I will answer you with gait and entrance. But we are
prevented.

[*Enter* **Olivia** *and* **Maria**]

80   Most excellent accomplished lady, the heavens rain odours
on you!

Sir Andrew   That youth's a rare courtier. 'Rain odours!'
Well.

Viola   My matter hath no voice, lady, but to your own most
85   pregnant and vouchsafed ear.

Sir Andrew   'Odours', 'pregnant', and 'vouchsafed'; I'll get
'em all three all ready.

Olivia   Let the garden door be shut, and leave me to my
hearing.

[*Exeunt* **Sir Toby, Sir Andrew**, *and* **Maria**]

90   Give me your hand, sir.

Viola   My duty, madam, and most humble service.

Sir Andrew I hope you are, sir. And I am yours.

Sir Toby [*heavily formal and wordily polite*] Will you cross the threshold? My niece desires you to enter, if you are on a trading visit to her.

Viola Yes, I am bound in the direction of your niece, sir. She is the purpose of my voyage.

Sir Toby Taste your legs, sir. Put them in motion.

Viola My legs under-stand me better than I understand what you mean by telling me to 'taste my legs'.

Sir Toby [*tersely*] I mean 'go in', sir: 'enter'.

Viola [*As she starts to walk in*] My gait is my reply, and also my entrance. [*She stops, seeing* **Olivia** *and* **Maria** *approach*] But we are anticipated!

[**Olivia** *and* **Maria** *come out of the house to meet her.* **Viola** *embarks on one of her very flamboyant prepared speeches*]

Most excellent and accomplished lady: may the heavens rain odours on you! [*She bows elaborately*]

Sir Andrew That youth's a splendid courtier. 'Rain odours'! Well!

Viola My message, lady, must be spoken only to your own most pregnant and vouchsafed ear.

Sir Andrew 'Odours', 'pregnant' and 'vouchsafed'. I must remember those three!

Olivia [*to her retinue*] Shut the garden door, and leave me to my private hearing.

[**Sir Toby, Sir Andrew** *and* **Maria** *leave*]

Give me your hand, sir. [*She offers hers*]

Viola [*taking it and bowing*] My duty to you madam, and most humble service.

Olivia   What is your name?

Viola   Cesario is your servant's name, fair princess.

Olivia   My servant, sir! 'Twas never merry world
95   Since lowly feigning was called compliment.
You're servant to the Count Orsino, youth.

Viola   And he is yours, and his must needs be yours;
Your servant's servant is your servant, madam.

Olivia   For him, I think not on him; for his thoughts,
100   Would they were blanks rather than filled with me!

Viola   Madam, I come to whet your gentle thoughts
On his behalf.

Olivia   O! by your leave, I pray you,
I bade you never speak again of him;
But, would you undertake another suit,
105   I had rather hear you to solicit that
Than music from the spheres.
Viola   Dear lady, –

Olivia   Give me leave, beseech you. I did send,
After the last enchantment you did here,
A ring in chase of you; so did I abuse
110   Myself, my servant, and, I fear me, you;
Under your hard construction must I sit,
To force that on you, in a shameful cunning,
Which you knew none of yours, what might you think?
Have you not set mine honour at the stake,
115   And baited it with all the unmuzzled thoughts
That tyrannous heart can think?
To one of your receiving, enough is shown;
A cypress, not a bosom, hides my heart.
So, let me hear you speak.

Viola   I pity you.

Olivia   What is your name?

Viola   Cesario is your servant's name, fair princess.

Olivia   *My* servant, sir? It's been a sad world since crawling was thought to be a compliment. You are the Count Orsino's servant, young man.

Viola   And he is yours. And what is his, of necessity must belong to you. Your servant's servant is *your* servant, madam.

Olivia   As for him, I don't think about him. As for his thoughts, I wish they were blanks rather than filled with me!

Viola   Madam, I'm here to make you more kindly disposed towards him.

Olivia   Oh, with respect, please: I asked you never to speak of him again. But if you insist on presenting another plea, I'd rather hear *you* doing it than heavenly music.

Viola   Dear lady –

Olivia   [*interrupting*] A word if I may. After your last bewitching visit here, I sent a ring after you. In doing so, I wronged myself, my servant, and, I fear, you. I must accept your condemnation for forcing something on you, in a shamefully devious way, which you knew wasn't yours. Whatever must you have thought? Have you not had cruel sport at the expense of my defenceless honour? [*She stops, blushing*] You've heard enough for someone of your intelligence. A thin veil, not my bosom, hides my heart.

Viola   I pity you.

120 **Olivia**   That's a degree to love.

Viola   No, not a grize; for 'tis a vulgar proof
That very oft we pity enemies.

Olivia   Why, then, methinks 'tis time to smile again.
O world! how apt the poor are to be proud.
125   If one should be a prey, how much the better
To fall before the lion than the wolf!

[*Clock strikes*]

The clock upbraids me with the waste of time.
Be not afraid, good youth, I will not have you;
And yet, when wit and youth is come to harvest,
130   Your wife is like to reap a proper man.
There lies your way, due west.

Viola   Then westward-ho!
Grace and good disposition attend your ladyship!
You'll nothing, madam, to my lord by me?

Olivia   Stay;
135   I prithee, tell me what thou think'st of me.

Viola   That you do think you are not what you are.

Olivia   If I think so, I think the same of you.

Viola   Then think you right; I am not what I am.

Olivia   I would you were as I would have you be!

140 **Viola**   Would it be better, madam, than I am?
I wish it might, for now I am your fool.

Olivia   O! what a deal of scorn looks beautiful
In the contempt and anger of his lip.
A murderous guilt shows not itself more soon
145   Than love that would seem hid; love's night is noon.
Cesario, by the roses of the spring,

Olivia   That's a step in love's direction.

Viola   Not even a small step. It's well known that we very often pity enemies.

Olivia   Well then, I think I'd better learn to smile again. Oh world! How proud the poor are! If one has to be a prey, how much better to be the victim of a lion rather than a mere wolf! [*A clock strikes*] The clock rebukes me for wasting time. Don't be afraid, good youth; you're not for me. Nevertheless, when your intelligence and youth reach their maturity, your wife will surely gain a first-rate man. There's your route: [*she points to the setting sun*] due west.

Viola   Then westward-ho! Blessing and a good life to your ladyship. You won't send a message to my lord, madam, through me?

Olivia   Stay a moment. May I ask you what you think of me?

Viola   [*Talking in riddles*] That you think you are what you are not. [*She means 'You think you are in love with a man, but you are not'*]

Olivia   [*assuming* **Viola** *is rudely suggesting she is proud*] If so, I think the same of you. [*That is, 'I think you are cheeky'*]

Viola   Then you are quite right. I am not what I am. [*'I'm a woman'*]

Olivia   [*also speaking in riddles*] I wish you were what I would like you to be. [*'My husband'*]

Viola   Would it be better, madam, than I am now? I hope so, because you are making me look very silly.

Olivia   [*to herself*] Oh, how handsome he looks when he is angry! Love that tries to hide itself is exposed even sooner than the crime of murder. Love is as plain as daylight, for all its secrecy. [*Aloud*] Cesario: by the roses of spring,

127

By maidhood, honour, truth, and every thing,
I love thee so, that, maugre all thy pride,
Nor wit nor reason can my passion hide.
150 Do not extort thy reasons from this clause,
For that I woo, thou therefore hast no cause;
But rather reason thus with reason fetter:
Love sought is good, but given unsought is better.

Viola   By innocence I swear, and by my youth,
155 I have one heart, one bosom, and one truth,
And that no woman has; nor never none
Shall mistress be of it, save I alone.
And so adieu, good madam; never more
Will I my master's tears to you deplore.

160 **Olivia**   Yet come again, for thou perhaps may'st move
That heart, which now abhors, to like his love.

[*Exeunt*]

Scene 2

Olivia's House. Enter **Sir Toby Belch, Sir Andrew Aguecheek** *and* **Fabian**

Sir Andrew   No, faith, I'll not stay a jot longer.

Sir Toby   Thy reason, dear venom; give thy reason.

Fabian   You must needs yield your reason, Sir Andrew.

Sir Andrew   Marry, I saw your niece do more favours to the
5   count's serving-man than ever she bestowed upon me; I saw't
i' the orchard.

maidenhood, honour, truth and everything – I love you so much that in spite of all your pride, neither common sense nor caution can conceal my passion. Don't deduce from this confession of love that because I'm wooing you, you therefore have something of no value. Far better to link common sense and expediency. Love that's sought after is good, but love that's given unasked is better.

Viola   In all innocence, and as I am a youth, I swear my heart, my loyalty and my integrity are as one, and that no woman has a share; nor shall one ever be mistress of it, except myself alone. So farewell, good madam. I'll never again plead on behalf of my tearful master.

Olivia   Do come again. You may perhaps be able to change my loathing for him to a liking.

[*They go*]

Scene 2

A room in Olivia's house. Enter **Sir Toby Belch, Sir Andrew Aguecheek** *and* **Fabian**

Sir Andrew   No indeed: I won't stay a moment longer.

Sir Toby   Your reason, dear crosspatch, give your reason!

Fabian   You've got to give us your reason, Sir Andrew.

Sir Andrew   Well, I saw your niece being nicer to the Count's servant than she has ever been to me. I saw it in the garden.

Sir Toby   Did she see thee the while, old boy? Tell me that.

Sir Andrew   As plain as I see you now.

Fabian   This was a great argument of love in her toward you.

10 **Sir Andrew**   Slight! will you make an ass o' me?

Fabian   I will prove it legitimate, sir, upon the oaths of judgement and reason.

Sir Toby   And they have been grand-jurymen since before Noah was a sailor.

15 **Fabian**   She did show favour to the youth in your sight only to exasperate you, to awake your dormouse valour, to put fire in your heart, and brimstone in your liver. You should then have accosted her, and with some excellent jests, fire-new from the mint, you should have banged the youth into
20 dumbness. This was looked for at your hand, and this was balked; the double gilt of this opportunity you let time wash off, and you are now sailed into the north of my lady's opinion, where you will hang like an icicle on a Dutchman's beard, unless you do redeem it by some laudable attempt,
25 either of valour or policy.

Sir Andrew   An't be any way, it must be with valour, for policy I hate; I had as lief be a Brownist as a politician.

Sir Toby   Why then, build me thy fortunes upon the basis of valour; challenge me the count's youth to fight with him; hurt
30 him in eleven places; my niece shall take note of it; and assure thyself, there is no lover-broker in the world can more prevail in man's commendation with woman than report of valour.

Fabian   There is no way but this, Sir Andrew.

35 **Sir Andrew**   Will either of you bear me a challenge to him?

Sir Toby   Did she see you at the time, old boy? Tell me that.

Sir Andrew   As plain as I can see you now.

Fabian   This was a clear proof of her love for you!

Sir Andrew   'Strewth, are you making me out to be an ass?

Fabian   I'll prove it right, sir, on grounds of common-sense and reason.

Sir Toby   That's been good enough for grand-jurymen since before Noah went to sea.

Fabian   She was nice to the youth in front of you just to exasperate you; to awaken your dormant valour; to put fire in your heart and brimstone in your liver. You should have tackled her then, and with some smart witticisms, all brand-new, you should have struck the youth dumb. This was expected of you, and you jibbed at it. You missed your chance of this golden opportunity, and now you're out in the cold, where you'll hang like an icicle on a Dutchman's beard if you don't put it right by some praiseworthy effort either of valour or clever policy.

Sir Andrew   If it has to be either way, it's got to be with valour, because I hate policy. I'd rather be one of those bible-punchers than a politician.

Sir Toby   Well, then, why don't you build up your fortunes on the basis of valour then? Challenge the Count's youth to a fight. Hurt him in eleven places. My niece will get to hear of it. Be assured, there's no matchmaker in the world more persuasive in commending a man to a woman than a report of valour.

Fabian   It's the only way, Sir Andrew . . .

Sir Andrew   Would either of you bear the challenge to him?

Sir Toby   Go, write it in a martial hand; be curst and brief; it
is no matter how witty, so it be eloquent and full of
invention; taunt him with the licence of ink; if thou thou'st
him some thrice, it shall not be amiss; and as many lies as
40   will lie in thy sheet of paper, although the sheet were big
enough for the bed of Ware in England, set 'em down; go,
about it. Let there be gall enough in thy ink, though thou
write with a goose-pen, no matter. About it.

Sir Andrew   Where shall I find you?

45 **Sir Toby**   We'll call thee at the cubiculo; go.

[*Exit* **Sir Andrew**]

Fabian   This is a dear manakin to you, Sir Toby.

Sir Toby   I have been dear to him, lad; some two thousand
strong or so.

Fabian   We shall have a rare letter from him; but you'll not
50   deliver it?

Sir Toby   Never trust me, then; and by all means stir on the
youth to an answer. I think oxen and wainropes cannot hale
them together. For Andrew, if he were opened, and you find
so much blood in his liver as will clog the foot of a flea, I'll
55   eat the rest of the anatomy.

Fabian   And his opposite, the youth, bears in his visage no
great presage of cruelty.

[*Enter* **Maria**]

Sir Toby   Look, where the youngest wren of nine comes.

Maria   If you desire the spleen, and will laugh yourselves into
60   stitches, follow me. Yond gull Malvolio is turned heathen, a

Sir Toby   Go, write it in aggressive handwriting. Be sharp and
to the point. It doesn't matter how smart it is, so long as it's
eloquent and inventive. Taunt him with all the advantages
of the written word. If you cheek him two or three times,
that'll be all right. And put down as many lies as you can tell
on a sheet of paper, however big it is: even if it were big
enough for the Great Bed of Ware in England, which is for
twelve people. Go on – do it. Let there be plenty of bitter
gall in your ink, even though your pen will be a white feather
from a goose; that doesn't matter. Off you go!

Sir Andrew   Where shall I find you?

Sir Toby   We'll call for you at the writing-room. Go!

[**Sir Andrew** *goes*]

Fabian   He's your dear little puppet, Sir Toby!

Sir Toby   I've been dear to him, lad: about two thousand
pounds or so.

Fabian   We shall have a choice letter from him. You won't
deliver it?

Sir Toby   Never trust me again, then! And I'll do my best to
provoke the youth to respond. I think oxen and tow-ropes
couldn't draw them together! As for Andrew, if you opened
him and found enough blood in him to clog the foot of a flea,
I'll eat the rest of him.

Fabian   And his opponent, the youth, has no great look of
ferocity about him!

[**Maria** *enters*]

Sir Toby   Look, here comes little jenny wren!

Maria   If you want to laugh yourselves sick and be in stitches,
follow me. That mug Malvolio has turned heathen; deserted

133

very renegado; for there is no Christian, that means to be
saved by believing rightly, can ever believe such impossible
passages of grossness. He's in yellow stockings!

Sir Toby   And cross-gartered?

65 **Maria**   Most villainously; like a pedant that keeps a school i'
the church. I have dogged him like his murderer. He does
obey every point of the letter that I dropped to betray him; he
does smile his face into more lines than is in the new map
with the augmentation of the Indies. You have not seen such
70   a thing as 'tis; I can hardly forbear hurling things at him. I
know my lady will strike him; if she do, he'll smile and take't
for a great favour.

Sir Toby   Come, bring us, bring us where he is.

[*Exeunt*]

Scene 3

A Street. Enter **Sebastian** *and* **Antonio**

Sebastian   I would not by my will have troubled you;
But since you make your pleasure of your pains,
I will no further chide you.

Antonio   I could not stay behind you; my desire,
5   More sharp than filed steel, did spur me forth;
And not all love to see you, though so much
As might have drawn one to a longer voyage,
But jealousy what might befall your travel,
Being skilless in these parts, which to a stranger,
10   Unguided and unfriended, often prove

his religion; no Christian who seeks salvation through the true faith can ever believe such incredibly vulgar deeds! He's in yellow stockings!

Sir Toby   And cross-gartered?

Maria   Hideously – like a teacher in a church school. I've stalked him as if I was after his life. He's obeyed every item in the letter that I dropped to trick him. He's got more lines on his face through smiling than there are on the latest map of the West Indies. You're never seen such a sight. I can hardly resist hurling things at him. I know my lady will hit him. If she does, he'll smile and take it as a great favour.

Sir Toby   Come on, take us – take us to where he is!

[*They hurry off*]

Scene 3

A street. Enter **Sebastian** *and* **Antonio**

Sebastian   It wasn't my intention to trouble you, but since you enjoy putting yourself out, I won't scold you any more.

Antonio   I couldn't stay behind. My wishes, sharper than pointed steel, urged me on. And it wasn't just a desire to see you – though I'd undertake a much longer voyage to do that – but worry as to what might happen to you: you being unfamiliar with this country, which can often prove rough and inhospitable to a stranger without a guide or friend. My

Rough and unhospitable; my willing love,
The rather by these arguments of fear,
Set forth in your pursuit.

Sebastian   My kind Antonio,
I can no other answer make but thanks,
15 And thanks, and ever thanks; and oft good turns
Are shuffled off with such uncurrent pay;
But, were my worth, as is my conscience, firm,
You should find better dealing. What's to do?
Shall we go see the relics of this town?

20 **Antonio**   Tomorrow, sir; best first go see your lodging.

Sebastian   I am not weary, and 'tis long to night.
I pray you, let us satisfy our eyes
With the memorials and the things of fame
That do renown this city.

Antonio   Would you'd pardon me;
25 I do not without danger walk these streets;
Once, in a sea-fight 'gainst the Count his galleys,
I did some service – of such note, indeed,
That were I ta'en here it would scarce be answered.

Sebastian   Belike you slew great number of his people.

30 **Antonio**   The offence is not of such a bloody nature,
Albeit the quality of the time and quarrel
Might well have given us bloody argument.
It might have since been answered in repaying
What we took from them; which, for traffic's sake,
35 Most of our city did; only myself stood out;
For which, if I be lapsed in this place,
I shall pay dear.

Sebastian   Do not then walk too open.

strong love for you, prompted by these fears for your safety, made me set off after you.

Sebastian   My kind Antonio: I can only answer you with thanks, more thanks, and even more thanks. Good turns are often discharged with that kind of useless currency! If I were as rich in money as I am in obligation to you, you'd be more handsomely rewarded. What shall we do? Shall we visit the sights of this town?

Antonio   Tomorrow, sir. Find your lodgings first, that's best.

Sebastian   I'm not tired, and it's still very early. Why not let us do some sightseeing round the monuments and places of historic interest that this city is renowned for?

Antonio   If I may be excused. I walk these streets in some danger. Once, in a sea-fight against the Count's ships, I played a part – so prominent, in fact, that if I were captured I'd stand no chance.

Sebastian   You killed many of his people?

Antonio   My offence was not of that sort, though the circumstances of the dispute might well have led to slaughter. It could be settled by repaying what we took from them, which, in the interests of trade, almost everyone in our city did. I stuck out. If I'm arrested in this place, I'll pay dearly for it.

Sebastian   Don't walk about so openly then.

Antonio   It doth not fit me. Hold, sir; here's my purse.
　　　In the south suburbs, at the Elephant,
40　Is best to lodge; I will bespeak our diet,
　　　Whiles you beguile the time and feed your knowledge
　　　With viewing of the town; there shall you have me.

Sebastian   Why I your purse?

Antonio   Haply your eye shall light upon some toy
45　You have desire to purchase; and your store,
　　　I think, is not for idle markets, sir.

Sebastian   I'll be your purse-bearer, and leave you for an
　　　hour.

Antonio   To the Elephant.

50 **Sebastian**   I do remember.

[*Exeunt*]

Scene 4

Olivia's Garden. Enter **Olivia** *and* **Maria**

Olivia   I have sent after him; he says he'll come,
　　　How shall I feast him? What bestow of him?
　　　For youth is bought more oft than begged or borrowed.
　　　I speak too loud.
5　Where is Malvolio? He is sad and civil,
　　　And suits well for a servant with my fortunes;
　　　Where is Malvolio?

Maria   He's coming, madam; but in very strange manner. He
　　　is, sure, possessed, madam.

138

Antonio   That's not like me. Here, sir, here's my purse. It's best to lodge in the south suburbs, at the Elephant Inn. I'll order our meal while you fill in the time and extend your education by viewing the town. You'll find me there.

Sebastian   Why give your purse to me?

Antonio   Perhaps you'll spot some souvenir you want to buy. I suspect you've little in reserve for buying luxuries.

Sebastian   I'll carry your purse, and leave you for an hour.

Antonio   To the Elephant . . .

Sebastian   I'll remember.

[*They go their separate ways*]

Scene 4

Olivia's garden. Enter **Olivia** *and* **Maria**

Olivia   [*to herself*] I've sent for him. If he says he'll come, how shall I entertain him, and what shall I give him? Youth is more often purchased than begged or borrowed. [*She realises* **Maria** *can hear her*] I'm speaking too loud. [*To* **Maria**] Where is Malvolio? He's serious and formal: very appropriate in a servant, considering my present predicament. Where is Malvolio?

Maria   He's coming madam, but behaving very oddly. I'm sure he's a bit touched, madam.

10 **Olivia**   Why, what's the matter? Does he rave?

Maria   No, madam; he does nothing but smile; your ladyship
were best to have some guard about you if he come, for sure
the man is tainted in's wits.

[*Exit* **Maria**]

Olivia   Go call him hither.
15   I am as mad as he,
        If sad and merry madness equal be.

[*Enter* **Maria** *and* **Malvolio**]

How now, Malvolio!

Malvolio   Sweet lady, ho, ho.

Olivia   Smilest thou?
20   I sent for thee upon a sad occasion.

Malvolio   Sad, lady! I could be sad; this does some obstruction
in the blood, this cross-gartering; but what of that? If it
please the eye of one, it is with me as the very true sonnet is,
'Please one, and please all'.

25 **Olivia**   Why, how dost thou, man? What is the matter with
thee?

Malvolio   Not black in my mind, though yellow in my legs. It
did come to his hands, and commands shall be executed; I
think we do know the sweet Roman hand.

30 **Olivia**   Wilt thou go to bed, Malvolio?

Malvolio   To bed! ay, sweetheart, and I'll come to thee.

Olivia   God comfort thee! Why dost thou smile so, and kiss
thy hand so oft?

Olivia   Why, what's the matter? Is he raving?

Maria   No, madam. He does nothing but smile. Your ladyship had better have a guard around you if he comes. I'm sure the man has lost his wits.

  Olivia   Go and bring him here.

[**Maria** *leaves, suppressing her laughter*]

I'm as mad as he is, if sad madness and merry madness are equal.

[**Maria** *enters with* **Malvolio**]

Greetings, Malvolio!

Malvolio   [*wreathed in his appalling smiles*] Sweet lady! [*winking heavily*] Ho, ho!

Olivia   Are you smiling? I sent for you because I am sad.

Malvolio   Sad, lady? I could be sad: this cross-gartering *does* restrict the blood supply – but who cares? If it is pleasing to 'someone' [*another knowing wink*] it suits me as the poem has it: 'Please one, please all'. [*More nudge-nudge, wink-wink*]

Olivia   Why, are you all right man? What's the matter with you?

Malvolio   Not full of black thoughts, though my legs *are* yellow. It *did* reach his hands; commands *shall* be carried out. [*Archly*] I think we recognize italic handwriting?

Olivia   [*concerned for his health*] Would you like to go to bed, Malvolio?

Malvolio   To bed? [*He blows several kisses at her*] Yes, sweetheart, and I'll come to you. [*The smile is like a shark's now*]

Olivia   God help you! Why are you smiling like that, and kissing your hand so often?

Maria   How do you, Malvolio?

35 **Malvolio**   At your request? Yes; nightingales answer daws.

Maria   Why appear you with this ridiculous boldness before my lady?

Malvolio   'Be not afraid of greatness'; 'twas well writ.

Olivia   What meanest thou by that, Malvolio?

40 **Malvolio**   'Some are born great,' –

Olivia   Ha!

Malvolio   'Some achieve greatness,' –

Olivia   What sayest thou?

Malvolio   'And some have greatness thrust upon them.'

45 **Olivia**   Heaven restore thee!

Malvolio   'Remember who commended thy yellow stockings,' –

Olivia   Thy yellow stockings!

Malvolio   'And wished to see thee cross-gartered.'

50 **Olivia**   Cross-gartered!

Malvolio   'Go to, thou art made, if thou desirest to be so;' –

Olivia   Am I made?

Malvolio   'If not, let me see thee a servant still.'

Olivia   Why, this is very midsummer madness.

[*Enter* **Servant**]

55 **Servant**   Madam, the young gentleman of the Count Orsino's is returned. I could hardly entreat him back; he attends your ladyship's pleasure.

Maria   [*humouring him*] How are you, Malvolio?

Malvolio   You presume to ask? Nightingales don't answer jackdaws.

Maria   Why do you appear before my lady with such ridiculous boldness?

Malvolio   [*to* **Olivia**] 'Don't be afraid of greatness'. Well put.

Olivia   What do you mean by that, Malvolio?

Malvolio   'Some are born great' –

Olivia   What?

Malvolio   'Some achieve greatness' –

Olivia   What's that you're saying?

Malvolio   'And some have greatness thrust upon them'.

Olivia   May heaven cure you!

Malvolio   'Remember who praised your yellow stockings' –

Olivia   Your yellow stockings?

Malvolio   'And wished to see you cross-gartered'.

Olivia   Cross-gartered!

Malvolio   'Right, then: you are made, if you want to be'.

Olivia   Me, 'made'?

Malvolio   'If not, stay a steward forever'.

Olivia   Why, this is midsummer madness indeed!

   [*A* **Servant** *enters*]

Servant   Madam, Count Orsino's young gentleman has returned. It was hard to persuade him to come back. He awaits your ladyship's pleasure.

Olivia   I'll come to him.

[*Exit* **Servant**]

60   Good Maria, let this fellow be looked to. Where's my cousin
Toby? Let some of my people have a special care of him; I
would not have him miscarry for the half of my dowry.

[*Exeunt* **Olivia** *and* **Maria**]

Malvolio   O, ho! do you come near me now? No worse man
than Sir Toby to look to me! This concurs directly with the
letter; she sends him on purpose that I may appear stubborn
65   to him; for she incites me to that in the letter. 'Cast thy
humble slough,' says she; 'be opposite with a kinsman, surly
with servants; let thy tongue tang with arguments of state; put
thyself into the trick of singularity'; and consequently sets
down the manner how; as, a sad face, a reverend carriage, a
70   slow tongue, in the habit of some air of note, and so forth. I
have limed her; but it is Jove's doing, and Jove make me
thankful! And when she went away now, 'Let this fellow be
looked to'; fellow! not Malvolio, nor after my degree, but
fellow. Why, everything adheres together, that no dram of a
75   scruple, no scruple of a scruple, no obstacle, no incredulous
or unsafe circumstance – What can be said? Nothing that
can be can come between me and the full prospect of my
hopes. Well, Jove, not I, is the doer of this, and he is to be
thanked.

[*Enter* **Maria**, *with* **Sir Toby Belch** *and* **Fabian**]

80   **Sir Toby**   Which way is he, in the name of sanctity? If all the
devils of hell be drawn in little, and Legion himself
possessed him, yet I'll speak to him.

Olivia   I'll come to him.

[*The* **Servant** *goes*]

Maria, dear: let this fellow [*she means* **Malvolio**] be seen to. Where's my cousin Toby? Some of my people must take special care of him. I wouldn't have him come to harm for half my dowry.

[**Olivia** *and* **Maria** *leave*]

Malvolio   Oh ho! So you're beginning to get the message? No less a man than Sir Toby to look after me! This is exactly in line with the letter. She is sending him on purpose so that I can be awkward with him. That's what she incites me to be in the letter. [*He examines it again*] 'Cast off your humble exterior', she says, 'be argumentative with a certain kinsman; surly with servants; let your speech be about lofty matters; be an individualist' . . . and then sets down how it should be done: for example, a serious face, a dignified walk, a slow manner of speech, clothes in the style of some nobleman of note, and so forth. I've got her! But it's Jove's doing, and may Jove make me thankful! And when she went away just now: 'Let this fellow be seen to' . . . Fellow! Not 'Malvolio', nor by my rank, but 'fellow'! Why, everything ties up. Not one grain of doubt, no grain of a grain, no obstacle, no impediment of any kind at all – what more can be said? – nothing that could ever happen can come between me and the fulfilment of my hopes. Well, Jove, not me, has done this, and he is to be thanked.

[**Maria** *re-enters, followed by* **Sir Toby Belch** *and* **Fabian**]

Sir Toby   Where is he, in the name of all that's holy? If all the devils in hell have concentrated together, and Lucifer himself possessed him, I'll speak to him.

Fabian   Here he is, here he is. How is't with you, sir?

Sir Toby   How is't with you, man?

85 **Malvolio**   Go off; I discard you; let me enjoy my private; go off.

Maria   Lo, how hollow the fiend speaks within him! Did not
I tell you? Sir Toby, my lady prays you to have a care of
him.

Malvolio   Ah ha! does she so?

90 **Sir Toby**   Go to, go to; peace! peace! We must deal gently
with him; let me alone. How do you, Malvolio? How is't
with you? What, man! defy the devil; consider, he's an enemy
to mankind.

Malvolio   Do you know what you say?

95 **Maria**   La you! an you speak ill of the devil, how he takes it at
heart. Pray God, he be not bewitched!

Fabian   Carry his water to the wise woman.

Maria   Marry, and it shall be done tomorrow morning if I
live. My lady would not lose him for more than I'll say.

100 **Malvolio**   How now, mistress!

Maria   O Lord!

Sir Toby   Prithee, hold thy peace; this is not the way; do you
not see you move him? Let me alone with him.

Fabian   No way but gentleness; gently, gently; the fiend is
105   rough, and will not be roughly used.

Sir Toby   Why, how now, my bawcock! how dost thou,
chuck?

Fabian   Here he is, here he is [*To* **Malvolio**] How are you, sir?

Sir Toby   How are you, man?

Malvolio   Go away. I reject you. Let me enjoy my privacy. Go away.

Maria   Look how deeply the fiend speaks from inside him! Didn't I tell you? Sir Toby, my lady wants you to treat him with care.

Malvolio   Ah ha! Does she really?

Sir Toby   [*to* **Maria** *and* **Fabian**] Leave off, leave off. Sh! Sh! We must deal with him gently. Leave it to me. [*He approaches* **Malvolio** *cautiously*] How do you do, Malvolio? How are things? What, man? Defy the devil! Remember, he's mankind's enemy!

Malvolio   [*pompously*] Do you know what you are saying?

Maria   [*to* **Sir Toby** *and* **Fabian**] Just notice! When you speak ill of the devil, see how personally he takes it. Pray God he isn't bewitched!

Fabian   Take a sample of his water to the quack!

Maria   Indeed, it'll be done tomorrow morning, upon my life. My lady wouldn't lose him for more money than I'd care to name! [*She approaches him*]

Malvolio   What, madam!

Maria   [*jumping back*] Oh Lord!

Sir Toby   Please, do be quiet. This isn't the way. Don't you see you are annoying him? Leave him to me.

Fabian   You must use gentleness. Gently! Gently! The devil is violent, and he won't be treated roughly!

Sir Toby   [*trying again*] Well, hello there, my cocksparrow! How are you, chick!

Malvolio Sir!

110 **Sir Toby** Ay, Biddy, come with me. What, man! 'tis not for
gravity to play at cherry-pit with Satan; hang him, foul
collier!

Maria Get him to say his prayers, good Sir Toby; get him to
pray.

Malvolio My prayers, minx!

115 **Maria** No, I warrant you, he will not hear of godliness.

Malvolio Go, hang yourselves all! You are idle, shallow
things; I am not of your element. You shall know more
hereafter.

[*Exit*]

Sir Toby Is't possible?

120 **Fabian** If this were played upon a stage now, I could
condemn it as an improbable fiction.

Sir Toby His very genius hath taken the infection of the
device, man.

Maria Nay, pursue him now, lest the device take air, and
125 taint.

Fabian Why, we shall make him mad indeed.

Maria The house will be the quieter.

Sir Toby Come, we'll have him in a dark room, and bound.
My niece is already in the belief that he's mad; we may carry
130 it thus, for our pleasure and his penance, till our very
pastime, tired out of breath, prompt us to have mercy on
him; at which time we will bring the device to the bar, and

Malvolio [*rising to his full height*] Sir!

Sir Toby [*offering to lead him away*] Yes, duckie, come with me. What, man! Sober citizens like you shouldn't be playing games with Satan. Hang him, foul devil from the underworld!

Maria Get him to say his prayers, good Sir Toby. Get him to pray!

Malvolio [*haughty in the extreme*] My prayers, minx?

Maria [*shaking her head wisely*] No, naturally: he won't hear of godliness.

Malvolio Go and hang yourselves, all of you! You are idle, good-for-nothings! I am not of your sort. You'll hear about this later.

[*He goes off, nose in the air*]

Sir Toby Is it possible?

Fabian If this were in a play I'd condemn it as an improbable fiction!

Sir Toby He's fallen for it hook, line and sinker, man!

Maria But do follow him at once, in case the joke has time to turn sour.

Fabian Why, we'll make him *really* mad.

Maria The house will be all the quieter!

Sir Toby I tell you what: we'll have him put in a dark room in a straightjacket. My niece already believes he's mad. We can pull this off – for our pleasure and his pains – till we get so tired of our game that we're prompted to have mercy on him. Then we'll make a clean breast of it, and you'll be

crown thee for a finder of madmen. But see, but see.

[*Enter* **Sir Andrew Aguecheek**]

Fabian   More matter for a May morning.

135 **Sir Andrew**   Here's the challenge; read it; I warrant there's
vinegar and pepper in't.

Fabian   Is't so saucy?

Sir Andrew   Ay, is't, I warrant him; do but read.

Sir Toby   Give me. [*Reading*] 'Youth, whatsoever thou art,
140   thou art but a scurvy fellow.'

Fabian   Good and valiant.

Sir Toby   'Wonder not, nor admire not in thy mind, why I do
call thee so, for I will show thee no reason for't.'

Fabian   A good note, that keeps you from the blow of the law.

145 **Sir Toby**   'Thou comest to the Lady Olivia, and in my sight
she uses thee kindly; but thou liest in thy throat, and that is
not the matter I challenge thee for.'

Fabian   Very brief, and to exceeding good sense-less.

Sir Toby   'I will waylay thee going home; where, if it be thy
150   chance to kill me, –'

Fabian   Good.

Sir Toby   'Thou killest me like a rogue and a villain.'

Fabian   Still you keep o' the windy side of the law; good.

crowned for your skill in finding madmen! [*He sees* **Sir Andrew** *approaching*] But see who's here!

[**Sir Andrew Aguecheek** *enters waving a piece of paper*]

Fabian   More matter for merrymaking!

Sir Andrew   Here's the challenge! Read it: I promise you there's vinegar and pepper in it.

Fabian   Is it so saucy?

Sir Andrew   [*missing the joke*] Yes, it is, to be sure. Just read it.

Sir Toby   Give it to me. [*He takes the letter and reads it*] '*Youth, whoever you are, you are a scurvy fellow.*'

Fabian   Good and valiant.

Sir Toby   '*Don't wonder, or be surprised in your mind, why I call you that, because I don't intend to give you a reason for it.*'

Fabian   [*solemnly*] A good touch. That keeps you inside the law.

Sir Toby   '*You visit the Lady Olivia, and in front of me she treats you kindly. But you lie in your teeth. That's not the reason why I'm challenging you.*'

Fabian   Very brief, and exceedingly good sense. [*Whispering aside*] – lessness!

Sir Toby   '*I will waylay you on your way home, when, if you are fortunate enough to kill me –*'

Fabian   Good.

Sir Toby   '*You'd be killing me like a rogue and a villain.*'

Fabian   [*wisely*] Still you keep on the right side of the law: good.

151

Sir Toby   'Fare thee well; and God have mercy upon one of
155   our souls! He may have mercy upon mine, but my hope is
better; and so look to thyself. Thy friend, as thou usest him,
and thy sworn enemy,

                                        Andrew Aguecheek'

If this letter move him not, his legs cannot. I'll give't him.

Maria   You may have very fit occasion for't; he is now in some
160   commerce with my lady, and will by and by depart.

Sir Toby   Go, Sir Andrew; scout me for him at the corner of
the orchard, like a bum-baily; so soon as ever thou seest him,
draw; and, as thou drawest, swear horrible; for it comes to
pass oft that a terrible oath, with a swaggering accent sharply
165   twanged off, gives manhood more approbation than ever
proof itself would have earned him. Away!

Sir Andrew   Nay, let me alone for swearing.

                                                    [*Exit*]

Sir Toby   Now will not I deliver his letter; for the behaviour
of the young gentleman gives him out to be of good capacity
170   and breeding; his employment between his lord and my niece
confirms no less; therefore this letter, being so excellently
ignorant, will breed no terror in the youth; he will find it
comes from a clodpole. But, sir, I will deliver his challenge
by word of mouth; set upon Aguecheek a notable report of
175   valour; and drive the gentleman, as I know his youth will
aptly receive it, into a most hideous opinion of his rage, skill,
fury, and impetuosity. This will so fright them both that
they will kill one another by the look, like cockatrices.

Sir Toby   *'Farewell, and God have mercy on one of our souls.*
He may have mercy on mine, but I think I have a better
chance. So think about it. Your friend, as you treat him, and
your sworn enemy,

Andrew Aguecheek.'

If this letter doesn't shift him, his legs can't. I'll give it to
him.

Maria   The time is just ripe for it: he's now conversing with my
lady and will depart by and by.

Sir Toby   Go, Sir Andrew. Keep a watch on him at the corner
of the garden like a warrant-officer. As soon as ever you see
him, draw your sword, and as you draw, swear
horribly − because very often a terrible oath spoken with
swaggering self-confidence does more for a man's
reputation than the actual fight would have earned him. [*He
gives* **Sir Andrew** *a push in the right direction*] Off you go!

Sir Andrew   You can leave the swearing to me.

[*He goes to take up his post*]

Sir Toby   [*to* **Fabian**] Now I won't deliver this letter: because
the behaviour of the young gentleman suggests he can look
after himself, and that he's of good breeding. His
employment as go-between confirms this. Therefore this
letter, being a masterpiece of ignorance, will generate no
terror in the youth. He'll know it comes from a blockhead.
Instead, sir, I'll deliver this challege by word of mouth. I'll
make Aguecheek out to be very brave, and drive the young
gentleman − who'll believe it all, being so young − into a
totally false idea of his anger, skill, fury and hotheadedness.
This will frighten them both so much that they'll kill one
another by exchanging looks, like those legendary
cockatrices are supposed to do.

Fabian   Here he comes with your niece; give them way till he
180   take leave, and presently after him.

Sir Toby   I will meditate the while upon some horrid message
for a challenge.

[*Exeunt* **Sir Toby**, **Fabian** *and* **Maria**]

[*Enter* **Olivia** *and* **Viola**]

Olivia   I have said too much unto a heart of stone,
And laid mine honour too unchary on't;
185   There's something in me that reproves my fault,
But such a headstrong potent fault it is
That it but mocks reproof.

Viola   With the same 'haviour that your passion bears,
Goes on my master's grief.

190   **Olivia**   Here; wear this jewel for me; 'tis my picture;
Refuse it not; it hath no tongue to vex you;
And I beseech you come again tomorrow.
What shall you ask of me that I'll deny,
That honour saved may upon asking give?

195   **Viola**   Nothing but this: your true love for my master.

Olivia   How with mine honour may I give him that
Which I have given to you?

Viola   I will acquit you.

Olivia   Well, come again tomorrow; fare you well;
A fiend like thee might bear my soul to hell.

[*Exit*]

[*Enter* **Sir Toby Belch** *and* **Fabian**]

200   **Sir Toby**   Gentleman, God save thee.

Fabian   Here he comes with your niece. Stand aside till he leaves, then immediately follow him.

Sir Toby   Meanwhile I'll give some thought to a horrid message for a challenge.

[**Sir Toby, Fabian** *and* **Maria** *go their separate ways*]

[**Olivia** *re-enters with* **Viola**]

Olivia   I've said too much to a heart of stone, and exposed my honour too indiscreetly. Something in me says I did wrong, but it's a fault so headstrong and so chronic that it's proof against rebuke.

Viola   My master's grief has the same quality as your passion.

Olivia   Here, wear this locket for me; inside is my picture. Don't refuse it: it has no tongue to vex you. And I beg you come again tomorrow. What could you ask of me that I would deny, provided it's honourable?

Viola   Nothing but this: your true love for my master.

Olivia   How could I honourably give him that, when I've given it to you?

Viola   I will release you.

Olivia   Well, come again tomorrow. Goodbye. A fiend like you could carry off my soul to hell.

[*She hurries off*]

[**Sir Toby Belch** *and* **Fabian** *re-enter*]

Sir Toby   Gentleman: God save you.

Viola   And you, sir.

Sir Toby   That defence thou hast, betake thee to't; of what
nature the wrongs are thou hast done him, I know not; but
thy intercepter, full of despite, bloody as the hunter, attends
205   thee at the orchard-end. Dismount thy tuck, be yare in thy
preparation, for thy assailant is quick, skilful, and deadly.

Viola   You mistake, sir; I am sure no man hath any quarrel to
me; my remembrance is very free and clear from any image of
offence done to any man.

210 **Sir Toby**   You'll find it otherwise, I assure you; therefore, if
you hold your life at any price, betake you to your guard; for
your opposite hath in him what youth, strength, skill, and
wrath can furnish man withal.

Viola   I pray you, sir, what is he?

215 **Sir Toby**   He is knight, dubbed with unhatched rapier, and
on carpet consideration; but he is a devil in private brawl;
souls and bodies hath he divorced three, and his incensement
at this moment is so implacable that satisfaction can be none
but by pangs of death and sepulchre. Hob, nob, is his word;
220   give't or take't.

Viola   I will return again into the house, and desire some
conduct of the lady: I am no fighter. I have heard of some
kind of men that put quarrels purposely on others to taste
their valour; belike this is a man of that quirk.

225 **Sir Toby**   Sir, no; his indignation derives itself out of a very
competent injury! Therefore get you on and give him his
desire. Back you shall not to the house, unless you undertake
that with me which with as much safety you might answer
him; therefore on, or strip your sword stark naked; for meddle
230   you must, that's certain, or forswear to wear iron about you.

Viola   This is as uncivil as strange. I beseech you, do me this

Viola   And you, sir.

Sir Toby   Whatever you have to defend yourself, get it ready. What kind of wrongs you've done him I don't know, but your challenger – full of fury, as bloodthirsty as a hunting-dog – is waiting for you at the bottom of the garden. Draw your sword; get ready with all speed; because your assailant is quick, skilful and deadly.

Viola   You must be mistaken, sir. I'm sure no man has any quarrel with me. My memory is completely free and clear of any recollection of offence done to any man.

Sir Toby   You'll find it otherwise, I assure you. Therefore, if you value your life, take up your guard. Your opposite has all the gifts of youth, strength, skill and anger.

Viola   Who is he, may I ask?

Sir Toby   He is a knight, dubbed with a ceremonial sword as he knelt on a carpet: but he's a devil in a private brawl. He's killed three people, and he's so incensed now that there's no satisfying him except through painful death and burial. 'Strike first' is his philosophy: take it or leave it.

Viola   I'll return to the house and ask the lady for protection. I'm no fighter. I've heard there are some men who provoke quarrels with others just to test their valour. Probably this is a man of that type.

Sir Toby   Sir, no! His anger stems from a very real cause. Therefore you'd better get on with it and give him his satisfaction. You shall not go back into the house, unless you cross swords with me, which would be no more safe than fighting him. Therefore proceed, or take your sword out now; because fight you must, that's for certain, or stop wearing a weapon on you.

Viola   This is as uncivil as it is strange. I beg you, do me this

courteous office, as to know of the knight what my offence to
him is; it is something of my negligence, nothing of my
purpose.

235 **Sir Toby**   I will do so. Signior Fabian, stay you by this
gentleman till my return.

[*Exit*]

Viola   Pray you, sir, do you know of this matter?

Fabian   I know the knight is incensed against you, even to a
mortal arbitrement, but nothing of the circumstance more.

240 **Viola**   I beseech you, what manner of man is he?

Fabian   Nothing of that wonderful promise, to read him by
his form, as you are like to find him in the proof of his
valour. He is indeed, sir, the most skilful, bloody, and fatal
opposite that you could possibly have found in any part of
245 Illyria. Will you walk towards him? I will make your peace
with him if I can.

Viola   I shall be much bound to you for't; I am one that had
rather go with sir priest than sir knight; I care not who knows
so much of my mettle.

[*Exeunt*]

[*Enter* **Sir Toby** *with* **Sir Andrew**]

250 **Sir Toby**   Why, man, he's a very devil; I have not seen such a
firago. I had a pass with him, rapier, scabbard, and all, and
he gives me the tuck-in with such a mortal motion that it is
inevitable; and on the answer, he pays you as surely as your
feet hit the ground they step on. They say he has been fencer
255 to the Sophy.

courtesy: may I know from the knight what I've done wrong
to him? It's something to do with an oversight; nothing
deliberate.

Sir Toby   I'll do so. Mister Fabian, stay by this gentleman till I
return.

[*He goes*]

Viola   [*trembling*] Sir, do you know about this matter, please?

Fabian   I know the knight is incensed against you, and that he
wants it settled in a fight to the death, but I don't know any
more about the details.

Viola   I beg of you: what kind of man is he?

Fabian   To look at him, there's none of that wonderful promise
which he shows when he's in action. He really is, sir, the
most skilful, bloody, and fatal opponent you could possibly
have found anywhere in Illyria. Will you walk towards him?
I'll make your peace with him if I can.

Viola   I'll be much obliged to you for it. I'm the kind of person
who'd rather go with Sir Priest than Sir Knight. I don't care
who knows that about my valour.

[*They go, with* **Viola** *very scared*]

[**Sir Toby** *and* **Sir Andrew** *re-enter*]

Sir Toby   Why, man, he's a very devil! I've never seen such a
firebrand. I had an exchange with him – rapier, scabbard,
the lot – and he gave me the stuck-in [*he demonstrates a
slick sword-thrust*] with such deadly accuracy that I couldn't
dodge it. On the return thrust, he strikes you as firmly as
your feet hit the ground they step on. They say he's been
fencer to the Shah of Persia.

Sir Andrew   Pox on't, I'll not meddle with him.

Sir Toby   Ay, but he will not now be pacified; Fabian can
scarce hold him yonder.

Sir Andrew   Plague on't; an I thought he had been valiant and
260   so cunning in fence I'd have seen him damned ere I'd have
challenged him. Let him let the matter slip, and I'll give him
my horse, grey Capilet.

Sir Toby   I'll make the motion. Stand here; make a good show
on't; this shall end without the perdition of souls. [*Aside*]
265   Marry, I'll ride your horse as well as I ride you.

[*Enter* **Fabian** *and* **Viola**]

I have his horse to take up the quarrel. I have persuaded him
the youth's a devil.

Fabian   He is as horribly conceited of him; and pants and
looks pale, as if a bear were at his heels.

270   **Sir Toby**   There's no remedy, sir; he will fight with you for's
oath sake. Marry, he hath better bethought him of his
quarrel, and he finds that now scarce to be worth talking of;
therefore draw for the supportance of his vow; he protests he
will not hurt you.

275   **Viola**   Pray God defend me! A little thing would make me tell
them how much I lack of a man.

Fabian   Give ground, if you see him furious.

Sir Toby   Come, Sir Andrew, there's no remedy; the
gentleman will, for his honour's sake, have one bout with
280   you; he cannot by the duello avoid it; but he has promised me,
as he is a gentleman and a soldier, he will not hurt you.
Come on; to't.

Sir Andrew   Dammit, I won't duel with him.

Sir Toby   Yes, but he won't be pacified now. Fabian can
scarcely keep him back over there.

Sir Andrew   Blast it, if I'd thought he was so brave and cunning
a fencer, I'd have seen him damned before I'd have
challenged him. If he'll cry off, I'll give him my horse, Grey
Capilet.

Sir Toby   I'll see what I can do. Stand here, do your best, and
this will end without a fatality. [*To himself*] Yes indeed, I'll
take your horse for a ride as well as you!

   [**Fabian** *and* **Viola** *enter*]

   [*To* **Fabian**] I've got his horse to settle the dispute. I've
persuaded him the youth's a devil.

Fabian   [*To* **Sir Toby**] He's just as frightened of Sir Andrew.
He's panting and has turned pale as if a bear was chasing
him.

Sir Toby   [*To* **Viola**] There's no remedy, sir. He'll fight you
because he's sworn to. Indeed he's now had second
thoughts about the quarrel, and now he thinks it was hardly
worth talking about. Therefore, draw in deference to his
vow. He swears he won't hurt you.

Viola   [*To herself*] Pray God defend me! I'm sorely tempted to
tell them that I'm not a man.

Fabian   [*To* **Viola**] Retreat if you see him furious.

Sir Toby   Come on, Sir Andrew: there's no remedy. For the
sake of his honour, the gentleman will have one bout with
you. By the rules of duelling he can't avoid it. But he has
promised me, as a gentleman and soldier, that he won't hurt
you. Come on – get going!

Sir Andrew   Pray God, he keep his oath! [*Draws his sword*]

Viola   I do assure you, 'tis against my will. [*Draws his sword*]

[*Enter* **Antonio**]

285 **Antonio**   Put up your sword. It this young gentleman
Have done offence, I take the fault on me;
If you offend him, I for him defy you. [*Draws his sword*]

Sir Toby   You, sir! Why, what are you?

Antonio   One, sir, that for his love dares yet do more
290   Than you have heard him brag to you he will.

Sir Toby   Nay, if you be an undertaker, I am for you. [*Draws
his sword*]

Fabian   O good Sir Toby, hold! Here come the officers.

[*Enter* **Officers**]

Sir Toby   I'll be with you anon.

Viola   Pray, sir, put your sword up, if you please.

295 **Sir Andrew**   Marry, will I, sir; and, for that I promised you,
I'll be as good as my word. He will bear you easily, and reins
well.

1st Officer   This is the man; do thy office.

2nd Officer   Antonio, I arrest thee at the suit
Of Count Orsino.

Sir Andrew   Pray God he keeps his word! [*He draws his sword nervously*]

Viola   I assure you, it's against my will. [*She draws her sword nervously, too*]
[**Viola** *and* **Sir Andrew** *close their eyes and swipe the air ineptly, weak at the knees.* **Antonio** *enters, and sees them apparently fighting. He thinks he sees* **Sebastian** *in trouble*]

Antonio   [*To* **Sir Andrew**] Put up your sword. If this young gentleman has offended you, I'll answer for him. If you've offended him, on his behalf I defy you! [*He draws his sword expertly*]

Sir Toby   You, sir! Why, who are you?

Antonio   Someone, sir, who for comrade's sake dares to do more than you have heard him boast to you he will.

Sir Toby   Well, if you're a substitute, I'm ready for you. [*He draws too*]

Fabian   [*Looking down the street*] Sir Toby, sir! Stop! Here come the officers of the law!

Sir Toby   I'll see you later! [*He puts his sword back quickly*]

Viola   [*To* **Sir Andrew**] Please, sir: put up your sword, please . . .

Sir Andrew   Indeed I will, sir, and I'll be as good as my word about my promise. Capulet will carry you comfortably, and responds well to the rein.

[*Two* **Officers** *enter*]

1st Officer   [*pointing to* **Antonio**] That's the man. Do your duty.

2nd Officer   Antonio, I arrest you on a summons of Count Orsino.

163

300 **Antonio**   You do mistake me, sir.

1st Officer   No, sir, no jot; I know your favour well,
Though now you have no sea-cap on your head.
Take him away; he knows I know him well.

Antonio   I must obey. [*To* **Viola**] This comes with seeking you;
305 But there's no remedy; I shall answer it.
What will you do, now my necessity
Makes me to ask you for my purse? It grieves me
Much more for what I cannot do for you
Than what befalls myself. You stand amazed;
310 But be of comfort.

2nd Officer   Come, sir, away.

Antonio   I must entreat of you some of that money.

Viola   What money, sir?
For the fair kindness you have showed me here,
315 And part, being prompted by your present trouble,
Out of my lean and low ability
I'll lend you something; my having is not much;
I'll make division of my present with you.
Hold, here is half my coffer.

Antonio   Will you deny me now?
320 Is't possible that my deserts to you
Can lack persuasion? Do not tempt my misery,
Lest that it make me so unsound a man
As to upbraid you with those kindnesses
That I have done for you.

Viola   I know of none;
325 Nor know I you by voice or any feature.
I hate ingratitude more in a man
Than lying, vainness, babbling drunkenness,
Or any taint of vice whose strong corruption
Inhabits our frail blood.

Antonio   You're making a mistake, sir.

1st Officer   No, sir, no way. I know your looks well, though
now you aren't wearing your sailor's cap. Take him away.
He knows I know him well.

Antonio   I'll go quietly. [*To* **Viola**] This comes from seeking
you. But there's no remedy: I'll have to answer for it. How
will you manage, now I'm driven to ask you for my purse
back? I'm far more upset about not being able to help you
than I am about my own fate. [**Viola** *looks thoroughly
baffled*] You look astonished, but be of good cheer.

2nd Officer   [*pulling* **Antonio** *away*] Come on, sir, away you
go.

Antonio   [*struggling to make his point first*] I must ask you for
some of that money.

Viola   What money, sir? For the genuine kindness you have
shown me here, and partly in response to your present
troubles, I'll lend you something from my slender resources. I
haven't got much; I'll share what I have with you. Here's
half my wealth.

Antonio   Will you refuse me now? Is it possible that what I've
done for you carries no weight? Don't provoke me in my
misery, in case I'm tempted to demean myself and reproach
you with my past kindnesses!

Viola   I don't know of any. Nor do I know you either by your
voice or by your looks. I hate ingratitude in a man more than
lying, boasting, babbling drunkenness, or any of the vices
that flesh is heir to.

Antonio   O heavens themselves!

330 **2nd Officer**   Come, sir, I pray you, go.

Antonio   Let me speak a little. This youth that you see here
I snatched one-half out of the jaws of death,
Relieved him with such sanctity of love,
And to his image, which methought did promise
335   Most venerable worth, did I devotion.

1st Officer   What's that to us? The time goes by; away!

Antonio   But O! how vile an idol proves this god!
Thou hast, Sebastian, done good feature shame.
In nature there's no blemish but the mind;
340   None can be called deformed but the unkind;
Virtue is beauty, but the beauteous evil
Are empty trunks o'erflourished by the devil.

1st Officer   The man grows mad; away with him! Come,
come, sir.

345 **Antonio**   Lead me on.

[*Exeunt* **Officers** *with* **Antonio**]

Viola   Methinks his words do from such passion fly,
That he believes himself; so do not I.
Prove true, imagination. O! prove true,
That I, dear brother, be now ta'en for you.

350 **Sir Toby**   Come hither, knight; come hither, Fabian; we'll
whisper o'er a couplet or two of most sage saws.

Viola   He named Sebastian; I my brother know
Yet living in my glass; even such and so
355   In favour was my brother; and he went
Still in this fashion, colour, ornament,

Antonio   [*unable to believe his ears*] Oh, sweet heaven!

2nd Officer   Come on, sir: off you go.

Antonio   Let me say something. This youth you see here, I
snatched half out of the jaws of death; aided him with a holy
love; and worshipped his very image, which I thought
worthy of reverence.

1st Officer   What's that to us? We're wasting time. Let's go.

Antonio   But oh, how wretched an idol this god proves to be!
Sebastian, you have brought shame upon your good looks.
There's no fault in nature worse than that of the mind. Only
the ungrateful can really be called 'deformed'. Virtue is
beautiful, but those who are beautiful to look at but evil
inside are empty boxes ornamented by the devil.

1st Officer   The man's mad. Away with him. Come on, sir,
come on . . .

Antonio   Take me away.

[*The* **Officers** *leave with* **Antonio** *as their prisoner*]

Viola   [*looking after him*] He speaks so passionately that I
think he believes himself. That's more than I do. [*An
explanation has begun to dawn on her*] May my thoughts
prove to be true! Oh, prove true – that I've been mistaken
for you, dear brother!

Sir Toby   [*to his companions*] Come here, knight; come here,
Fabian. We'll exchange a few wise words together . . .

Viola   He called me Sebastian . . . I know from my mirror that
we look exactly alike. [*Pointing to features of her face*] My
brother looked just like this, and this. And he dressed in this
fashion – [*pointing to her clothes*] the same colour and

> For him I imitate. O! if it prove,
> Tempests are kind, and salt waves fresh in love.

[*Exit*]

Sir Toby   A very dishonest paltry boy, and more a coward
360   than a hare. His dishonesty appears in leaving his friend here
in necessity, and denying him; and for his cowardship, ask
Fabian.

Fabian   A coward, a most devout coward, religious in it.

Sir Andrew   'Slid, I'll after him again, and beat him.

365 **Sir Toby**   Do; cuff him soundly, but never draw thy sword.

Sir Andrew   An I do not, –

[*Exit*]

Fabian   Come, let's see the event.

Sir Toby   I dare lay any money 'twill be nothing yet.

[*Exeunt*]

design, because I imitated him. Oh, if it's true, tempests are kindly, and salt waves full of love!

[*She goes off, full of hope*]

Sir Toby   A very dishonest, contemptible boy, and more cowardly than a hare. His dishonesty is demonstrated by his leaving his friend here in need, and denying he knows him. As for his cowardice – ask Fabian!

Fabian   He's a coward, a really *devout* coward. Fanatical!

Sir Andrew   'Strewth, I'll chase him again, and beat him!

Sir Toby   Do. Box his ears. But don't draw your sword!

Sir Andrew   [*all courage now*] If I don't –

[*The rest of his brave words are lost as he goes off*]

Fabian   Come on, let's see the result.

Sir Toby   I'll lay any money on it, nothing will happen.

[*They go*]

Act four

Scene 1

Before Olivia's House. Enter **Sebastian** *and* **Feste**

Feste   Will you make me believe that I am not sent for you?

Sebastian   Go to, go to; thou are a foolish fellow;
Let me be clear of thee.

Feste   Well held out, i'faith! No, I do not know you; nor I am
5   not sent to you by my lady to bid you come speak with her;
nor your name is not Master Cesario; nor this is not my nose
neither. Nothing that is so is so.

Sebastian   I prithee, vent thy folly somewhere else;
Thou know'st not me.

10 **Feste**   Vent my folly! He has heard that word of some great
man, and now applies it to a fool. Vent my folly! I am afraid
this great lubber, the world, will prove a cockney. I prithee
now, ungird thy strangeness and tell me what I shall vent to
my lady. Shall I vent to her that thou art coming?

15 **Sebastian**   I prithee, foolish Greek, depart from me;
There's money for thee; if you tarry longer
I shall give worse payment.

Feste   By my troth, thou hast an open hand. These wise men
that give fools money get themselves a good report – after
20   fourteen years' purchase.

[*Enter* **Sir Andrew**]

Act four

Scene 1

The street outside Olivia's house. Enter **Sebastian** *and* **Feste**

Feste   Are you trying to make out I wasn't looking for you?

Sebastian   Really, really! You are a foolish fellow. Do go away!

Feste   You're keeping this up very well! [*Sarcastically*] Oh no, I don't know you! Nor have I been sent by my lady to ask you to come and speak to her; nor is your name Cesario; nor is this [*he points to it*] my nose, either! Nothing that is so, is so!

Sebastian   Please. Give vent to your folly somewhere else. You don't know me.

Feste   [*mocking*] 'Give vent to my folly'! He's heard that word used by some great man, and now he applies it to a fool. 'Give vent to my folly'! I'm afraid this great noddy, the world, will also turn out to be a hollow sham. [*With heavy irony*] I beg you now, 'desist from your aloofness' and tell me what I'm to 'vent' to my lady? Shall I 'vent' to her that you are coming?

Sebastian   Please, you zany idiot, leave me alone. [*Taking out his purse*] There's some money for you. If you stay any longer I'll give you something worse!

Feste   Upon my word, you're very generous. Wise men who give money to fools get themselves well thought of – after payment over fourteen years!

[**Sir Andrew** *enters. He thinks he has found* **Viola**]

Sir Andrew   Now, sir, have I met you again? There's for you.
[*Striking* **Sebastian**]

Sebastian   Why, there's for thee, and there, and there.
[*Beating* **Sir Andrew**] Are all the people mad?

[*Enter* **Sir Toby** *and* **Fabian**]

Sir Toby   Hold, sir, or I'll throw your dagger o'er the house.
[*They seize* **Sebastian**]

25 **Feste**   This will I tell my lady straight. I would not be in
some of your coats for twopence.

Sir Toby   Come on, sir; hold.

Sir Andrew   Nay, let him alone; I'll go another way to work
with him; I'll have an action of battery against him if there be
30   any law in Illyria. Though I struck him first, yet it's no
matter for that.

Sebastian   Let go thy hand.

Sir Toby   Come, sir, I will not let you go. Come, my young
soldier, put up your iron; you are well fleshed; come on.

35 **Sebastian**   I will be free from thee. What would'st thou now?
If thou dar'st tempt me further, draw thy sword.

Sir Toby   What, what! Nay, then I must have an ounce or
two of this malapert blood from you.

[*Enter* **Olivia**]

Sir Andrew   Now, sir! So we meet again? That's for you! [*He strikes* **Sebastian**]

Sebastian   [*Striking back*] And that for you! And that! And that! Is everyone here mad?

[**Sir Toby** *and* **Fabian** *enter, and see* **Sir Andrew** *being beaten, as they think, by* **Viola**]

Sir Toby   Stop that, sir, or I'll throw your dagger over the house!

[*They seize* **Sebastian**]

Feste   I'll tell my lady about this straight away. I wouldn't be in your shoes for tuppence!

Sir Toby   Come with us, sir! [**Sebastian** *tries to free himself*] Stay still!

Sir Andrew   [*holding his sore head*] No, leave him alone! I'll get at him another way. I'll take out an action of battery against him, if there's any law in Illyria. Though I struck him first, that doesn't matter.

Sebastian   [*to* **Sir Toby**] Let go your hand!

Sir Toby   Come, sir: I won't let you go. Come on, my young soldier, arm yourself. You've had some experience. Come on!

Sebastian   [*struggling clear*] I will be free from you! [*He steps back and faces them*] Now, how about it? If you dare provoke me any further, draw your sword!

Sir Toby   What, what! Well then, I must have an ounce or two of your cheeky blood!

[*He draws his sword*]

[**Olivia** *enters*]

173

Olivia   Hold, Toby! On thy life I charge thee, hold!

40 **Sir Toby**   Madam!

Olivia   Will it be ever thus? Ungracious wretch!
Fit for the mountains and the barbarous caves,
Where manners ne'er were preached. Out of my sight!
Be not offended, dear Cesario.
Rudesby, be gone!

[*Exeunt* **Sir Toby, Sir Andrew** *and* **Fabian**]

45   I prithee, gentle friend,
Let thy fair wisdom, not thy passion, sway
In this uncivil and unjust extent
Against thy peace. Go with me to my house,
And hear thou there how many fruitless pranks
50 This ruffian hath botched up, that thou thereby
May'st smile at this. Thou shalt not choose but go;
Do not deny. Beshrew his soul for me,
He started one poor heart of mine in thee.

Sebastian   What relish is in this? How runs the stream?
55 Or I am mad, or else this is a dream.
Let fancy still my sense in Lethe steep;
If it be thus to dream, still let me sleep!

Olivia   Nay; come, I prithee; would thou'dst be ruled by me!

Sebastian   Madam, I will.

Olivia   O! say so, and so be.

[*Exeunt*]

Olivia Stop, Toby! Upon your life, I order you to stop!

Sir Toby [*shamefaced*] Madam . . .

Olivia Must it always be the same? You uncouth wretch, fit only for the mountains and barbarous caves where manners were never taught! Get out of my sight! [*To* **Sebastian,** *mistaking him for* **Viola**] Don't be offended, Cesario. [*Turning to* **Sir Toby,** *who has hesitated before obeying her order*] Barbarian! Be off with you!

[**Sir Toby, Sir Andrew** *and* **Fabian** *leave in disgrace*]

Please, my gentle friend: let your commonsense, rather than your anger, govern how you react to this uncivil and unjust attack upon your peace. Go with me to my house and I'll tell you there how many pointless pranks this ruffian has thought up. That way you'll maybe smile at this one. [**Sebastian** *is naturally hesitant*] I insist you come. Don't say no. Shame on his soul – he gave my half of your heart a shock.

Sebastian [*totally mystified, especially by the last cryptic remark*] What does all this mean? What's the idea? Either I'm mad, or else this is a dream. [*Looking at* **Olivia,** *and recognizing the strength of her feeling for him*] Let me remain oblivious. If this is dreaming, let me sleep on!

Olivia Please come with me! I wish you'd do as I tell you . . .

Sebastian [*still dazed*] Madam, I will.

Olivia [*delighted*] Oh, just say that, and you'll be obeying orders!

[*They leave*]

Scene 2

Olivia's House. Enter **Maria** *and* **Feste**

Maria   Nay, I prithee, put on this gown and this beard; make
him believe thou art Sir Topas the curate; do it quickly; I'll call
Sir Toby the whilst.

[*Exit*]

Feste   Well, I'll put it on, and I will dissemble myself in't; and
5   I would I were the first that ever dissembled in such a gown.
I am not tall enough to become the function well, nor lean
enough to be thought a good student; but to be said an honest
man and a good housekeeper goes as fairly as to say a careful
man and a great scholar. The competitors enter.

[*Enter* **Sir Toby Belch** *and* **Maria**]

10   **Sir Toby**   Jove bless thee, Master Parson.

Feste   Bonos dies, Sir Toby; for, as the old hermit of Prague,
that never saw pen and ink, very wittily said to a niece of
King Gorboduc, 'That that is is'; so I, being Master Parson,
am Master Parson, for what is 'that' but 'that', and 'is' but
15   'is'?

Sir Toby   To him, Sir Topas.

Feste   What ho! I say. Peace in this prison.

Sir Toby   The knave counterfeits well; a good knave.

Malvolio   Who calls there?

Scene 2

A room in Olivia's house. Enter **Maria** *who is carrying a clerical gown and a false beard, and* **Feste**

Maria   Now then, put on this gown and this beard to make him believe you are Sir Topas, the parson. Hurry! I'll call Sir Toby in the meantime.

Feste   Well, I'll put it on and disguise myself in it. I wish I were the first one to wear a clerical gown to cover deceit! I'm not distinguished enough to look the part, or thin enough to be thought a good student, but to be called a decent man and a good host is as commendable as being a frugal man and a great scholar. The conspirators enter . . .

[**Sir Toby Belch** *and* **Maria** *join him*]

Sir Toby   God bless you, Master Parson.

Feste   [*acting the part of a solemn and learned cleric*] Good day, Sir Toby. [*Making up a series of fictions*] As the old hermit of Prague, who never used pen and ink, very wittily said to a niece of King Gorboduc: 'That that is, is.' So I, being Master Parson, *am* Master Parson; because what is the meaning of 'that' other than 'that', and 'is' other than 'is'?

Sir Toby   [*indicating a door with a small grille in it to permit conversation*] Tackle him, Sir Topas!

Feste   [*speaking through the grille in his clerical voice*] Hello there, I say! God's peace in this prison!

Sir Toby   The rogue impersonates well. He's a good rogue.

Malvolio   [*from the other side of the door, pitifully*] Who's calling?

20 **Feste**   Sir Topas the curate, who comes to visit Malvolio the
lunatic.

Malvolio   Sir Topas, Sir Topas, good Sir Topas, go to my
lady.

Feste   Out, hyperbolical fiend! How vexest thou this man!
25   Talkest thou nothing but of ladies?

Sir Toby   Well said, Master Parson.

Malvolio   Sir Topas, never was man thus wronged. Good Sir
Topas, do not think I am mad; they have laid me here in
hideous darkness.

30 **Feste**   Fie, thou dishonest Satan! I call thee by the most
modest terms; for I am one of those gentle ones that will use
the devil himself with courtesy. Sayest thou that house is
dark?

Malvolio   As hell, Sir Topas.

35 **Feste**   Why, it hath bay windows transparent as barricadoes,
and the clerestories toward the south-north are as lustrous as
ebony; and yet complainest thou of obstruction?

Malvolio   I am not mad, Sir Topas. I say to you, this house is
dark.

40 **Feste**   Madman, thou errest; I say there is no darkness but
ignorance, in which thou art more puzzled than the
Egyptians in their fog.

Malvolio   I say this house is as dark as ignorance, though
ignorance were as dark as hell; and I say there was never man
45   thus abused. I am no more mad than you are; make the trial
of it in any constant question.

Feste   What is the opinion of Pythagoras concerning wild
fowl?

Feste   Sir Topas, the parson, who comes to visit Malvolio the
lunatic.

Malvolio   Sir Topas, Sir Topas, good Sir Topas: go to my lady.

Feste   [*exorcizing the devil*] Out with you, hyper-diabolical
fiend! How you torment this man! [*To* **Malvolio**] Can you talk
of nothing but *ladies*? [*He tuts disapprovingly*]

Sir Toby   Well said, Master Parson!

Malvolio   Sir Topas, never was a man so wronged. Good Sir
Topas, do not think I'm mad. They've put me here in
hideous darkness.

Feste   Fie on you, dishonest Satan – I'm calling you by the
most moderate of terms because I'm one of those gentle
people who would treat the devil himself courteously – are
you saying that place is dark?

Malvolio   As hell, Sir Topas.

Feste   Why, it has bay windows, transparent as shutters, and
the high windows towards the south-north are as bright as
ebony: and yet you are complaining that the light is blocked?

Malvolio   I'm not mad, Sir Topas. I tell you, this place is dark.

Feste   Madman, you are in error. I say there is no darkness but
ignorance, in which you are more enveloped than the
Egyptians in the bible were by their fog.

Malvolio   I tell you this place is as dark as ignorance, the kind
that's as black as hell. And I tell you there never was a man
so badly treated. I am no more mad than you are. Test me by
asking some searching questions.

Feste   What is the opinion of Pythagoras concerning wild
fowl?

Malvolio   That the soul of our grandam might haply inhabit
50   a bird.

Feste   What thinkest thou of his opinion?

Malvolio   I think nobly of the soul, and no way approve his
opinion.

Feste   Fare thee well; remain thou still in darkness. Thou shalt
55   hold the opinion of Pythagoras ere I will allow of thy wits,
and fear to kill a woodcock, lest thou dispossess the soul of
thy grandam. Fare thee well.

Malvolio   Sir Topas! Sir Topas!

Sir Toby   My most exquisite Sir Topas!

60 **Feste**   Nay, I am for all waters.

Maria   Thou might'st have done this without thy beard and
gown; he sees thee not.

Sir Toby   To him in thine own voice, and bring me word
how thou findest him. I would we were well rid of this
65   knavery. If he may be conveniently delivered, I would he
were; for I am now so far in offence with my niece that I
cannot pursue with any safety this sport to the upshot. Come
by and by to my chamber.

[*Exeunt* **Sir Toby** *and* **Maria**]

Feste   [*Singing*]   *Hey Robin, jolly Robin,*
70   *Tell me how thy lady does.*

Malvolio   Fool!

Feste   *My lady is unkind, perdy.*

Malvolio   Fool!

180

Malvolio   That the soul of one's grandmother might possibly inhabit a bird.

Feste   What do you think of his opinion?

Malvolio   I think that the soul is noble, and no way agree with his opinion.

Feste   Fare you well. Remain in darkness. You must share the opinion of Pythagorus before I will certify you sane, and be afraid of killing a woodcock for fear of displacing the soul of your granny. Fare you well.

Malvolio   Sir Topas! Sir Topas!

Sir Toby   My most exquisite Sir Topas!

Feste   [*to Sir Toby*] I'm very versatile!

Maria   You could have done this without your beard and gown. He can't see you.

Sir Toby   Go to him now in your own voice, and come and tell me how you find him. [*To **Maria***] I wish we were well rid of this practical joking. If he can be conveniently set free, I would he were, as I'm now so out of favour with my niece that I can't see this hoax through to its end with any safety. Come to my room by and by.

[**Sir Toby** *and* **Maria** *exit*]

Feste   [*himself now, pretending to be passing by **Malvolio**'s door, singing*]

> Hey Robin, jolly Robin,
> Tell me how my lady does!

Malvolio   Fool!

Feste   *My lady is indeed unkind.*

Malvolio   [*louder*] Fool!

181

Feste   *Alas! why is she so?*

Malvolio   Fool, I say!

Feste   *She loves another.*

                                    Who calls, ha?

75 **Malvolio**   Good fool, as ever thou wilt deserve well at my
hand, help me to a candle, and pen, ink, and paper. As I am
a gentleman, I will live to be thankful to thee for't.

Feste   Master Malvolio!

Malvolio   Ay, good fool.

Feste   Alas, sir, how fell you besides your five wits?

80 **Malvolio**   Fool, there was never man so notoriously abused; I
am as well in my wits, fool, as thou art.

Feste   But as well? Then you are mad indeed, if you be no
better in your wits than a fool.

Malvolio   They have here propertied me; keep me in
85   darkness, send ministers to me, asses! and do all they can to
face me out of my wits.

Feste   Advise you what you say; the minister is here [*As* **Sir
Topas**] Malvolio, Malvolio, thy wits the heavens restore!
Endeavour thyself to sleep, and leave thy vain bibble-babble.

90 **Malvolio**   Sir Topas!

Feste   Maintain no words with him, good fellow. [*As* **Feste**]
Who, I, sir? Not I, sir. God be wi' you, good Sir Topas. [*As*
Sir Topas] Marry, amen . . . [*As* **Feste**] I will, sir, I will.

Malvolio   Fool, fool, fool, I say!

95 **Feste**   Alas, sir, be patient. What say you, sir? I am shent for
speaking to you.

Feste   *Alas, why is she so?*

Malvolio   [*louder still*] Fool, I say!

Feste   *She loves another.*
   Who's that calling, eh?

Malvolio   Good fool, if you want to do yourself some good by
   me, get me a candle and pen, ink and paper. As I'm a gentleman, I'll live to show my thanks to you for it.

Feste   Master Malvolio!

Malvolio   Yes, good fool.

Feste   Alas, sir: how do you come to be insane?

Malvolio   Fool, there never was a man so shamefully abused.
   I'm as sane, fool, as you are.

Feste   Only as sane? Then you are mad indeed if you're no
   more sane than a fool.

Malvolio   They have put me away here; kept me in darkness;
   sent parsons to me – the asses! – and they do all they can
   to drive me out of my wits.

Feste   Take care what you say. The parson is here! [*In his* **Sir
   Topas** *voice*] Malvolio, Malvolio, may heaven restore your
   wits! Try to sleep, and leave off your pointless
   gobbledegook!

Malvolio   Sir Topas!

Feste   [*still* **Sir Topas**] Don't talk to him, good fellow. [*His own
   voice*] Who, I, sir? Not me, sir. God be with you, good Sir
   Topas. [**Sir Topas** *again*] Yes indeed. Amen. [*His own voice*]
   I will sir, I will.

Malvolio   Fool, fool, I say!

Feste   Alas, sir, be patient. What do you want? I'm in trouble
   for speaking to you.

Malvolio   Good fool, help me to some light and some paper; I
tell thee I am as well in my wits as any man in Illyria.

Feste   Well-a-day, that you were, sir!

100 **Malvolio**   By this hand, I am. Good fool, some ink, paper,
and light; and convey what I will set down to my lady; it shall
advantage thee more than ever the bearing of letter did.

Feste   I will help you to't. But tell me true, are you not mad
indeed, or do you but counterfeit?

105 **Malvolio**   Believe me, I am not; I tell thee true.

Feste   Nay, I'll ne'er believe a madman till I see his brains. I
will fetch you light and paper and ink.

Malvolio   Fool, I'll requite it in the highest degree; I prithee,
be gone.

110 **Feste**   [*Singing*]   *I am gone, sir,*
And anon, sir,
I'll be with you again,
In a trice
Like to the old Vice,
115   *Your need to sustain;*

Who with dagger of lath,
In his rage and his wrath,
Cries, Ah, ha! to the devil;
Like a mad lad,
120   *Pare thy nails, dad;*
Adieu, goodman devil.

[*Exit*]

Malvolio   Good fool, help me to get some light and some
paper. I tell you I'm as sane as any man in Illyria.

Feste   Would that you were, sir.

Malvolio   By this hand, I am. Good fool: some ink, paper and
light – and take what I write to my lady. It will profit you
more than the delivery of any other letter ever did.

Feste   I'll help you. But tell me the truth. Are you really mad, or
are you pretending?

Malvolio   Believe me, I am not. I'm telling you the truth.

Feste   No: I'll never believe a madman till I see his brains. I'll
fetch you light and paper and ink.

Malvolio   Fool, I'll reward it handsomely. Please go now.

Feste   [*singing*]   *I am gone, sir,*
And anon, sir,
I'll be with you again,
In a trice
Like Old Vice,
Your need to sustain;

Who with dagger of lath,
In his rage and his wrath,
Cries Ah, ha! to the devil;
Like a mad lad,
Pare thy nails, dad;
Adieu, mister devil!

[*He goes*]

185

Scene 3

Olivia's Garden. Enter **Sebastian**

Sebastian   This is the air; that is the glorious sun;
      This pearl she gave me, I do feel't and see't;
      And though 'tis wonder that enwraps me thus,
      Yet 'tis not madness. Where's Antonio then?
5   I could not find him at the Elephant;
      Yet there he was, and there I found this credit,
      That he did range the town to seek me out.
      His counsel now might do me golden service;
      For though my soul disputes well with my sense
10   That this may be some error, but no madness,
      Yet doth this accident and flood of fortune
      So far exceed all instance, all discourse,
      That I am ready to distrust mine eyes,
      And wrangle with my reason that persuades me
15   To any other trust but that I am mad
      Or else the lady's mad; yet if 'twere so,
      She could not sway her house, command her followers,
      Take and give back affairs and their dispatch
      With such a smooth, discreet, and stable bearing
20   As I perceive she does. There's something in't
      That is deceivable. But here the lady comes.

[*Enter* **Olivia** *and a* **Priest**]

  Olivia   Blame not this haste of mine. If you mean well,
25   Now go with me and with this holy man
      Into the chantry by; there, before him,
      And underneath that consecrated roof,
      Plight me the full assurance of your faith,
      That my most jealous and too doubtful soul

Scene 3

Olivia's garden. Enter **Sebastian** *who still can't believe he's awake*

Sebastian   This is the air. . . . That's the glorious sun. This pearl the lady gave me — I can feel it and see it. . . . And though I'm filled with amazement, it's certainly not madness. Where's Antonio, then? I couldn't find him at the Elephant Inn. He'd been there, and there I was informed he's roamed the town trying to find me. His advice now might be worth its weight in gold. Though my mind argues convincingly against my commonsense, saying all this could be an error, but not madness — yet this accidental encounter with good fortune is so unusual, so contrary to reason, that I'm ready to distrust my eyes, and argue with my mind when it tries to persuade me to any conclusion other than that I'm mad — or else my lady is mad. Yet if she *were* mad, she couldn't rule her house, command her servants, manage business matters and their discharge, with such a smooth, discreet and confident manner as I observe she does. There's something in this I don't understand. But here comes the lady.

[*Enter* **Olivia** *and* **Priest**]

Olivia   Do not blame me for this haste. If you mean well, go with me and this holy man into the nearby chapel. There, before him, and beneath that consecrated roof, pledge me your vows of love in marriage, so my most jealous and suspicious soul may live at peace. He'll keep it secret till you

May live at peace. He shall conceal it
Whiles you are willing it shall come to note,
30 What time we will our celebration keep
According to my birth. What do you say?

Sebastian I'll follow this good man, and go with you;
And, having sworn truth, ever will be true.

Olivia Then lead the way, good father; and heavens so shine
35 That they may fairly note this act of mine!

[*Exeunt*]

are willing to make it public, and then we'll have a wedding celebration in keeping with my rank. What do you say?

Sebastian   I'll follow this good man and go with you, and having sworn to be true, I shall be ever more.

Olivia   Then lead the way good father, and may heaven's blessing endorse my actions!

[*They go*]

Act five

Scene 1

Before Olivia's House. Enter **Feste** *and* **Fabian**

Fabian Now, as thou lovest me, let me see his letter.

Feste Good Master Fabian, grant me another request.

Fabian Anything.

Feste Do not desire to see this letter.

5 **Fabian** This is, to give a dog, and in recompense desire my dog again.

[*Enter* **Duke, Viola, Curio,** *and* **Attendants**]

Duke Belong you to the Lady Olivia, friends?

Feste Ay, sir; we are some of her trappings.

Duke I know thee well; how dost thou, my good fellow?

10 **Feste** Truly, sir, the better for my foes and the worse for my friends.

Duke Just the contrary; the better for thy friends.

Feste No, sir, the worse.

Duke How can that be?

15 **Feste** Marry, sir, they praise me and make an ass of me; now my foes tell me plainly I am an ass; so that by my foes, sir, I profit in the knowledge of myself, and by my friends I am abused; so that, conclusions to be as kisses, if your four

Act five

Scene 1

The street in front of Olivia's house. Enter **Feste** *and* **Fabian**

Fabian   Now do me a favour and let me see his letter.

Feste   Dear Master Fabian, grant me another request.

Fabian   Anything.

Feste   Don't ask to see this letter.

Fabian   That's like making a present of a dog, then in recompense asking for it back again!

[*The* **Duke, Viola, Curio** *and* **Attendants** *enter*]

Duke   Are you Lady Olivia's men, friends?

Feste   Yes, sir; we are part of her outfit.

Duke   [*recognizing him*] I know you well. How are you, my good fellow?

Feste   Truly, sir: all the better for having enemies, and all the worse for having friends.

Duke   On the contrary: all the better for having friends.

Feste   No, sir, the *worse*.

Duke   How can that be?

Feste   Well, sir, they praise me, which makes me an ass. Now my foes tell me bluntly that I *am* an ass. So through my foes, sir, I know myself better, and by my friends, I'm deceived. So, comparing this with kisses, if four negatives [*he means*

191

20   negatives make your two affirmatives, why then, the worse
for my friends and the better for my foes.

Duke   Why, this is excellent.

Feste   By my troth, sir, no; though it please you to be one of
my friends.

Duke   Thou shalt not be the worse for me; there's gold.

25 **Feste**   But that it would be double-dealing, sir, I would you
could make it another.

Duke   O! you give me ill counsel.

Feste   Put your grace in your pocket, sir, for this once, and let
your flesh and blood obey it.

30 **Duke**   Well, I will be so much a sinner to be a double-dealer;
there's another.

Feste   Primo, secundo, tertio, is a good play; and the old
saying is, the third pays for all; the triplex, sir, is a good
tripping measure; or the bells of Saint Bennet, sir, may put
35   you in mind: one, two, three.

Duke   You can fool no more money out of me at this throw; if
you will let your lady know I am here to speak with her, and
bring her along with you, it may awake my bounty further.

Feste   Marry, sir, lullaby to your bounty till I come again. I
40   go, sir; but I would not have you to think that my desire of
having is the sin of covetousness; but as you say, sir, let your
bounty take a nap; I will awake it anon.

[*Exit*]

lips] make two positives, [*two mouths kissing, or one kiss*]
why then I'm the worse for having friends, and the better
for having foes.

Duke   Very clever!

Feste   Upon my word, sir, I'm not; though you are so kind as
to be one of my friends.

Duke   You mustn't be worse off on my account. Here's gold.
[*He gives him a coin*]

Feste   That would be deceit, sir: double dealing. I wish you
could give me another.

Duke   Oh, you give me bad advice!

Feste   Just for this once, put your pride in your pocket and
just follow your inclinations.]*He holds out his hand*]

Duke   [*giving him a second coin*] Well, I'll sin to the extent of
being a double-dealer. There's another.

Feste   [*rattling the two coins together*] 'One, two, three' is
good for starting something; and there's the old saying
'third time lucky'; three beats to a bar is good for dancing
to; or perhaps the bells of St Bennet's Church, sir, might
remind you: [*he speaks the words like a striking clock*] One:
two: three . . .?

Duke   You can't fool any more money out of me now, but if
you'll let your lady know I'm here to speak to her, and bring
her back with you, it might re-awaken my generosity.

Feste   Well sir, may your generosity sleep well till I return. I go,
sir. But I wouldn't want you to think that my desire to have
is the sin of covetousness. But as you say, sir, let your
generosity take a nap. I will awaken it soon.

[*He goes*]

Viola   Here comes the man, sir, that did rescue me.

[*Enter* **Antonio** *and* **Officers**]

Duke   That face of his I do remember well;
45   Yet, when I saw it last, it was besmeared
As black as Vulcan in the smoke of war.
A baubling vessel was he captain of,
For shallow draught and bulk unprizable;
With which such scathful grapple did he make
50   With the most noble bottom of our fleet,
That very envy and the tongue of loss
Cried fame and honour on him. What's the matter?

1st Officer   Orsino, this is that Antonio
That took the Phoenix and her fraught from Candy;
55   And this is he that did the Tiger board,
When your young nephew Titus lost his leg.
Here in the streets, desperate of shame and state,
In private brabble did we apprehend him.

Viola   He did me kindness, sir, drew on my side;
60   But in conclusion put strange speech upon me;
I know not what 'twas but distraction.

Duke   Notable pirate! thou salt-water thief!
What foolish boldness brought thee to their mercies,
Whom thou, in terms so bloody and so dear,
Hast made thine enemies?

65 **Antonio**   Orsino, noble sir,
Be pleased that I shake off these names you give me;
Antonio never yet was thief or pirate,
Though I confess, on base and ground enough,
Orsino's enemy. A witchcraft drew me hither;
70   That most ungrateful boy there by your side,
From the rude sea's enraged and foamy mouth

Viola   Here comes the man who rescued me, sir.

[**Antonio** *and the* **Officers** *enter*]

Duke   I remember that face of his well, but when I last saw it,
it was begrimed like Vulcan's with the smoke of war. He
was captain of an insignificant ship, not worth much
because of its shallow draught and small size. So
aggressively did he grapple with the finest ship in our fleet
that even those who hated him and suffered loss proclaimed
his fame and honour. What has he done?

1st Officer   Orsino, this is the Antonio who captured the
Phoenix and her cargo from Crete. The same fellow who
boarded the *Tiger* when your young nephew Titus lost his
leg. We arrested him here in the streets, indifferent to his
notoriety and danger, engaged in a private brawl.

Viola   He did me a kindness, sir, by drawing his sword to
defend me. Afterwards, he said some peculiar things to me.
As I could make no sense of it, I assumed it was madness.

Duke   Famous pirate, thief of the high seas! What
foolhardiness brought you to the mercy of those whom
you've made your enemies, through bloodshed and death?

Antonio   Orsino, noble sir: allow me to refute these names you
give me. I've never been a thief or pirate, though I confess
I've been your enemy for very good reasons. I was drawn
here by witchcraft. I saved that most ungrateful boy there by
your side from the stormy sea. He was a wreck past hope. I

Did I redeem; a wreck past hope he was;
His life I gave him, and did thereto add
My love, without retention or restraint,
75   All his in dedication; for his sake
Did I expose myself, pure for his love,
Into the danger of this adverse town;
Drew to defend him when he was beset;
Where being apprehended, his false cunning,
80   Not meaning to partake with me in danger,
Taught him to face me out of his acquaintance,
And grew a twenty-years-removed thing
While one would wink; denied me mine own purse,
Which I had recommended to his use
Not half an hour before.

85 **Viola**   How can this be?

Duke   When came he to this town?

Antonio   Today, my lord; and for three months before,
No interim, not a minute's vacancy
Both day and night did we keep company.

[*Enter* **Olivia** *and* **Attendants**]

90 **Duke**   Here comes the countess; now heaven walks on earth!
But for thee, fellow: fellow, thy words are madness;
Three months this youth hath tended upon me;
But more of that anon. Take him aside.

Olivia   What would my lord, but that he may not have,
95   Wherein Olivia may seem serviceable?
Cesario, you do not keep promise with me.

Viola   Madam?

Duke   Gracious Olivia –

Olivia   What do you say, Cesario? Good my lord, –

gave him his life, and added to it my love – unconditionally
and unreservedly – to use in his service. For his sake I
exposed myself to the dangers of this hostile town, entirely
out of love. I drew to defend him when he was attacked,
and when I was arrested, his false cunning led him to deny
his friendship to my face, because he'd no intention of
sharing danger with me. In the time it takes to blink, he'd
turned into someone who'd not seen me for twenty years.
He denied me my own purse, which I'd persuaded him to
use not half an hour before.

Viola   [*astonished*] How can this be?

Duke   [*to the* **Officers**] When did he arrive here in the town?

Antonio   [*answering for himself*] Today, my lord, and for the
past three months we've been together day and night,
without a break of so much as a minute.

[**Olivia** *enters with her* **Attendants**]

Duke   Here comes the Countess. Now heaven walks on earth!
[*To* **Antonio**] As for you, fellow: fellow, your words are
madness. For the past three months this youth has been my
servant. But more of that later. [*To the* **Officers**] Take him to
one side.

Olivia   [*to* **Orsino**] What does my lord desire, other than what
he cannot have, that Olivia can supply? [*She sees* **Viola** *who
she thinks is her new husband*] Cesario, you are not keeping
your promise to me.

Viola   [*puzzled yet again*] Madam?

Duke   Gracious Olivia –

Olivia   What did you say, Cesario? [*She sees* **Orsino** *about to
reply and checks him*] Please, my lord –

100 **Viola**   My lord would speak; my duty hushes me.

Olivia   If it be aught to the old tune, my lord,
It is as fat and fulsome to mine ear,
As howling after music.

Duke   Still so cruel?

Olivia   Still so constant, lord.

105 **Duke**   What, to perverseness? You uncivil lady,
To whose ingrate and unauspicious altars
My soul the faithfull'st offerings hath breathed out
That e'er devotion tendered! What shall I do?

Olivia   Even what it please my lord, that shall become him.

110 **Duke**   Why should I not, had I the heart to do it,
Like to the Egyptian thief at point of death,
Kill what I love? A savage jealousy
That sometimes savours nobly. But hear me this:
Since you to non-regardance cast my faith,
115 And that I partly know the instrument
That screws me from my true place in your favour,
Live you the marble-breasted tyrant still;
But this your minion, whom I know you love,
And whom, by heaven I swear, I tender dearly,
120 Him will I tear out of that cruel eye,
Where he sits crowned in his master's spite.
[*To* **Viola**] Come, boy, with me; my thoughts are ripe in
      mischief;
I'll sacrifice the lamb that I do love,
125 To spite a raven's heart within a dove.

Viola   And I, most jocund, apt, and willingly,
To do you rest, a thousand deaths would die.

Olivia   Where goes Cesario?

Viola   My lord wishes to speak. Duty demands that I stay
silent.

Olivia   [*to* **Orsino**] If you are back on your old theme, my lord,
it appeals to my ear like howling does after hearing music.

Duke   Still so cruel?

Olivia   Still so consistent, lord.

Duke   What, perverseness? You discourteous lady, at whose
ungrateful and unresponsive altars my soul has spoken the
most faithful prayers that ever were offered in devotion! [*He
wrings his hands in distress*] What shall I do?

Olivia   Whatever my lord wishes to do: that will suit him well.

Duke   If I had the courage to do it, shouldn't I kill what I love,
like the Egyptian brigand who tried to take his loved one
with him to the after-life? That was a savage sort of
heartache that had a touch of nobility about it! But listen to
this: since you scornfully refuse to recognize my love, and
because I think I know what has removed me from my
proper place in your favour, carry on being the cold and
stony-hearted tyrant that you are! But this darling of yours,
whom I know you love, and who – I swear by heaven – I
regard most tenderly: I'll tear him from that cruel eye of
yours where he's enthroned instead of me. [*Turning to*
Viola] Come with me, boy. I have some uncharitable
thoughts in my mind: I'll sacrifice the lamb I love [*he means*
Viola] to spite the raven's heart that lives within a dove. [*He
means* **Olivia**]

Viola   And I will die a thousand deaths, blithely, readily and
willingly if it will give you peace of mind. [*She makes to go*]

Olivia   Where is Cesario going?

Viola   After him I love
More than I love these eyes, more than my life,
130   More, by all mores, than e'er I shall love wife.
If I do feign, you witnesses above,
Punish my life for tainting of my love!

Olivia   Ay me, detested! how am I beguiled!

Viola   Who does beguile you? Who does do you wrong?

135   **Olivia**   Hast thou forgot thyself? Is it so long?
Call forth the holy father.

Duke   Come away!

Olivia   Whither, my lord? Cesario, husband, stay.

Duke   Husband!

Olivia   Ay, husband; can he that deny?

Duke   Her husband, sirrah!

Viola   No, my lord, not I.

140   **Olivia**   Alas! it is the baseness of thy fear
That makes thee strangle thy propriety.
Fear not, Cesario; take thy fortunes up;
Be that thou know'st thou art, and then thou art
As great as that thou fear'st.

[*Enter* **Priest**]

                                     O welcome, father!
145   Father, I charge thee, by thy reverence,
Here to unfold, though lately we intended
To keep in darkness what occasion now
Reveals before 'tis ripe, what thou dost know
Hath newly passed between this youth and me.

150   **Priest**   A contract of eternal bond of love,
Confirmed by mutual joinder of your hands,

Viola   After the man I love more than my eyes, more than my life: more than I shall ever love a wife, by far! You gods above, if I'm shamming, punish me for defiling my loved one!

Olivia   [*thinking she has been jilted*] Alas, how I'm despised! How I've been misled!

Viola   Who's misled you? Who's done you wrong?

Olivia   Have you forgotten yourself? Is it so long? Call the holy father here.

Duke   [*pulling* **Viola** *by the sleeve*] Come away!

Olivia   [*pulling* **Viola** *by the other one*] Where, my lord? Cesario, my husband: stay!

Duke   [*astounded*] Husband?

Olivia   Yes, husband. Can he deny it?

Duke   [*to* **Viola**] Her husband, sir?

Viola   No, my lord, not me!

Olivia   Alas, it's cowardly fear that's making you deny your own identity. Don't be afraid, Cesario. Take possession of your good fortune. Be what you know you are: then you are as great as him you fear.

[*The* **Priest** *enters*]

Welcome, Father! Father, I ask you as you are a holy man – notwithstanding our intention to keep dark what circumstances prematurely have revealed – to describe all you know about what has recently occurred between this youth and me.

Priest   A contract eternally binding you in love: confirmed by your holding each other's hands, proven by a holy kiss,

Attested by the holy close of lips,
Strengthened by interchangement of your rings;
And all the ceremony of this compact
155   Sealed in my function, by my testimony;
Since when, my watch hath told me, toward my grave
I have travelled but two hours.

Duke   O thou dissembling cub! what wilt thou be
When time hath sowed a grizzle on thy case?
160   Or will not else thy craft so quickly grow
That thine own trip shall be thine overthrow?
Farewell, and take her; but direct thy feet
Where thou and I henceforth may never meet.

Viola   My lord, I do protest, –

Olivia   O! do not swear;
165   Hold little faith, though thou hast too much fear.

[*Enter* **Sir Andrew Aguecheek**]

Sir Andrew   For the love of God, a surgeon! Send one
presently to Sir Toby.

Olivia   What's the matter?

Sir Andrew   He has broke my head across, and has given Sir
170   Toby a bloody coxcomb too. For the love of God, your help!
I had rather than forty pound I were at home.

Olivia   Who has done this, Sir Andrew?

Sir Andrew   The count's gentleman, one Cesario; we took him
for a coward, but he's the very devil incardinate.

175 **Duke**   My gentleman, Cesario?

Sir Andrew   'Od's lifelings! here he is. You broke my head
for nothing! And that that I did, I was set on to do't by
Sir Toby.

strengthened by the exchange of rings, with all the ceremonies of this agreement sealed by me as priest, and by myself as witness. This was only two hours ago, according to my watch.

Duke [*to* **Viola**, *fiercely*] Oh, you deceitful cub! What will you be like by the time your hair turns grey? Or will your craftiness develop so quickly that you'll trip yourself up? Farewell, and take her. But be sure our paths never cross in the future!

Viola My lord, I swear –

Olivia Oh, do not swear! Keep some of your honour intact, though you *are* so full of fear.

[**Sir Andrew Aguecheek** *enters*]

Sir Andrew For the love of God, a surgeon! Send one to Sir Toby immediately!

Olivia What's the matter?

Sir Andrew He's split my skull and given Sir Toby a cut head, too. For the love of God, help us! I'd give forty pounds to be at home.

Olivia Who has done this, Sir Andrew?

Sir Andrew The Count's gentleman, that Cesario fellow. We thought he was a coward, but he's the devil himself!

Duke My man Cesario?

Sir Andrew [*noticing* **Viola** *for the first time*] Strewth, here he is! [*To* **Viola**] You broke my head for nothing! And what I did, Sir Toby made me do!

Viola   Why do you speak to me? I never hurt you;
180   You drew your sword upon me without cause;
But I bespake you fair, and hurt you not.

Sir Andrew   If a bloody coxcomb be a hurt, you have hurt me;
I think you set nothing by a bloody coxcomb.

[*Enter* **Sir Toby** *and* **Feste**]

Here comes Sir Toby halting; you shall hear more; but if he
185   had not been in drink he would have tickled you othergates
than he did.

Duke   How now, gentlemen! how is't with you?

Sir Toby   That's all one; has hurt me, and there's the end
on't. Sot, didst see Dick Surgeon, sot?

190   **Feste**   O! he's drunk, Sir Toby, an hour agone; his eyes were
set at eight i' the morning.

Sir Toby   Then he's a rogue, and a passy-measures pavin. I
hate a drunken rogue.

Olivia   Away with him! Who hath made this havoc with
195   them?

Sir Andrew   I'll help you, Sir Toby, because we'll be dressed
together.

Sir Toby   Will you help? An ass-head, and a coxcomb, and a
knave, a thin-faced knave, a gull!

200   **Olivia**   Get him to bed, and let his hurt be looked to.

[*Exeunt* **Feste, Fabian, Sir Toby** *and* **Sir Andrew**]

[*Enter* **Sebastian**]

Sebastian   I am sorry, madam, I have hurt your kinsman;
But had it been the brother of my blood,

Viola   Why speak to me? I didn't hurt you. You drew your sword on me for no reason. But I was polite with you, and I didn't hurt you.

Sir Andrew   If a bloody head is a hurt, you *have* hurt me. I think you think a bloody head is nothing!

[*Enter* **Sir Toby Belch**, *drunk and supported by* **Feste**]

Here comes Sir Toby, limping. He'll have something to say. If he hadn't been drunk he'd have sorted you out better than he did!

Duke   [*to* **Sir Toby**] Well now, gentleman! How are you?

Sir Toby   [*waving his injury off*] That's neither here nor there. He's hurt me, and that's that. [*To* **Feste**] Clot, did you see Dick the surgeon, clot?

Feste   Oh, he's been drunk, Sir Toby, an hour since. His eyes were closed at eight this morning.

Sir Toby   Then he's a rogue and a staggering totterer! I hate a drunken rogue! [*Sir Toby staggers and totters as he speaks*]

Olivia   Take him away! Who has done this to them?

Sir Andrew   I'll help you, Sir Toby, because our wounds can be dressed together.

Sir Toby   [*rounding on him*] What, *you* help? An ass-head? An idiot? A knave? A thin-faced *simpleton*!

Olivia   Get him to bed, and see that his injuries are treated.

[**Feste, Fabian, Sir Toby** *and* **Sir Andrew** *leave*]

[**Sebastian** *enters. He addresses* **Olivia**, *his new wife*]

Sebastian   I'm sorry, madam, that I've hurt your kinsman; but had he been my own brother I could have done no less to

I must have done no less with wit and safety.
You throw a strange regard upon me, and by that
205   I do perceive it hath offended you;
Pardon me, sweet one, even for the vows
We made each other but so late ago.

Duke   One face, one voice, one habit, and two persons;
A natural perspective, that is, and is not!

210 **Sebastian**   Antonio! O my dear Antonio!
How have the hours racked and tortured me
Since I have lost thee!

Antonio   Sebastian are you?

Sebastian   Fear'st thou that, Antonio?

Antonio   How have you made division of yourself?
215   An apple cleft in two is not more twin
Than these two creatures. Which is Sebastian?

Olivia   Most wonderful!

Sebastian   Do I stand there? I never had a brother;
Nor can there be that deity in my nature,
220   Of here and everywhere. I had a sister,
Whom the blind waves and surges have devoured.
Of charity, what kin are you to me?
What countryman, what name, what parentage?

Viola   Of Messaline; Sebastian was my father;
225   Such a Sebastian was my brother too,
So went he suited to his watery tomb.
If spirits can assume both form and suit
You come to fright us.

Sebastian   A spirit I am indeed;
But am in that dimension grossly clad
230   Which from the womb I did participate.

secure my safety. [*He notices he is getting strange looks*]
You're looking at me oddly; I can tell it has offended you.
Forgive me, sweetest, on the strength of the vows we made
each other so recently.

Duke [*totally amazed*] One face. One voice. One style of
dress. And two persons! A human optical illusion,
something that is, yet isn't!

Sebastian [*seeing his old friend*] Antonio! Oh my dear
Antonio! How agonizing the hours have been since losing
you!

Antonio Are you – Sebastian?

Sebastian Are you in doubt, Antonio?

Antonio How have you managed to split yourself? Two halves
of an apple are not more alike than these two creatures. [*He
looks first at* **Viola,** *then at* **Sebastian**] Which is Sebastian?

Olivia Amazing!

Sebastian [*looking at* **Viola**] Am I standing there? I never had
a brother . . . nor do I have the divine gift of being here and
everywhere. I did have a sister, drowned in the cruel sea.
[*To* **Viola**] Would you be so kind: what relation are you to
me? What's your country; what's your name; who were your
parents?

Viola I'm from Messaline. Sebastian was my father's name,
and it was my brother's too. This was how he was dressed
when he was drowned. If ghosts can assume both the body
and the clothes, you've come to frighten us.

Sebastian I am a ghost indeed, but of the material world into
which I was born. If you were a woman, since everything

Were you a woman, as the rest goes even,
I should my tears let fall upon your cheek,
And say 'Thrice welcome, drowned Viola!'

Viola   My father had a mole upon his brow.

235 **Sebastian**   And so had mine.

Viola   And died that day when Viola from her birth
Had numbered thirteen years.

Sebastian   O! that record is lively in my soul.
He finished indeed his mortal act
240   That day that made my sister thirteen years.

Viola   If nothing lets to make us happy both,
But this my masculine usurped attire,
Do not embrace me till each circumstance
Of place, time, fortune, do cohere and jump
245   That I am Viola; which to confirm,
I'll bring you to a captain in this town,
Where lie my maiden weeds; by whose gentle help
I was preserved to serve this noble count.
All the occurrence of my fortune since
250   Hath been between this lady and this lord.

Sebastian   So comes it, lady, you have been mistook,
But nature to her bias drew in that.
You would have been contracted to a maid;
Nor are you there, by my life, deceived.
255   You are betrothed both to a maid and man.

Duke   Be not amazed; right noble is his blood.
If this be so, as yet the glass seems true,
I shall have share in this most happy wreck.
Boy, thou hast said to me a thousand times
260   Thou never should'st love woman like to me.

Viola   And all those sayings will I over-swear,

else fits in, I'd shed my tears upon your cheek and say 'Welcome, welcome, welcome, drowned Viola!'

Viola   My father had a mole on his brow.

Sebastian   Mine had, too.

Viola   And died when Viola was thirteen years old.

Sebastian   The memory is vivid in my soul. He died indeed on the day my sister was thirteen.

Viola   If there's no impediment to our mutual happiness other than these masculine clothes I've presumed to wear, don't embrace me till every detail of place, time and chance comes together to prove that I'm Viola. To confirm everything, I'll take you to a captain in this town; my woman's clothes are at his house. It was through his kind help that I was saved, to serve this noble Count. All my life since has been devoted to this lady, and this lord.

Sebastian   [*to Olivia*] That's how you've come to be mistaken, lady; but nature has turned it to your advantage. You would have been married to a woman, so you've avoided that, upon my life. Now you are married both to a virgin *and* a man!

Duke   Don't be alarmed: he's of noble blood. If all this is true, and so far there's no sign of it all being done by mirrors, I'll have a share in this most fortunate of shipwrecks. [*To* **Viola**] Boy, you have said to me a thousand times that you'd never love a woman as much as you love me.

Viola   All those sayings I will swear again, and all those

And all those swearings keep as true in soul
As doth that orbed continent the fire
That severs day from night.

Duke   Give me thy hand;
265   And let me see thee in thy woman's weeds.

Viola   The captain that did bring me first on shore
Hath my maid's garments; he upon some action
Is now in durance at Malvolio's suit,
A gentleman, and follower of my lady's.

270 **Olivia**   He shall enlarge him. Fetch Malvolio hither.
And yet, alas, now I remember me,
They say, poor gentleman, he is much distract.
A most extracting frenzy of mine own
From my remembrance clearly banished his.

[*Enter* **Feste**, *with a letter, and* **Fabian**]

275   How does he, sirrah?

Feste   Truly, madam, he holds Belzebub at the stave's end as
well as a man in his case may do. Has here writ a letter to you;
I should have given it you today morning; but as a madman's
epistles are no gospels, so it skills not much when they are
280   delivered.

Olivia   Open't, and read it.

Feste   Look then to be well edified when the fool delivers the
madman. [*Reads*] By the Lord, madam, –

Olivia   How now! art thou mad?

285 **Feste**   No, madam, I do but read madness; an your ladyship
will have it as it ought to be, you must allow vox.

Olivia   Prithee, read i' thy right wits.

swearings honour as faithfully as the sun does its task of
changing night to day.

Duke   Give me your hand, and let me see you in your woman's
dress.

Viola   The captain who first brought me ashore has my
dresses. He's under arrest over some legal matter which
Malvolio – a gentleman and servant of my lady's – has
initiated.

Olivia   He will set him free. Fetch Malvolio here. But
alas – I've just remembered. They say he's mentally
disturbed, poor gentleman; preoccupation with my own
mental distress clearly drove from my mind all recollection
of his.

[**Feste** *returns with a letter, followed by* **Fabian**]

[*To* **Feste**] How is he, fellow?

Feste   Well, madam, he keeps the devil at bay as well as a
man in his situation can do. He has written this letter to you:
I should have given it to you this morning, but as the epistles
of madmen aren't gospels, it doesn't matter much what day
they are delivered.

Olivia   Open it, and read it.

Feste   Expect your mind to be much improved when the fool
speaks what the madman writes: [*He assumes a zany sort of
voice*] 'By the Lord, madam' –

Olivia   What, are you mad too?

Feste   No, madam, I'm only reading madness. If your ladyship
wants it spoken as it should be, you must allow for some
interpretation.

Olivia   Please: read it as though you were in your right mind.

211

Feste   So I do, madonna; but to read his right wits is to read
thus; therefore perpend, my princess, and give ear.

290 **Olivia**   [*To* **Fabian**] Read it you, sirrah.

Fabian   [*Reading*] 'By the Lord, madam, you wrong me, and
the world shall know it; though you have put me into
darkness, and given your drunken cousin rule over me, yet
have I the benefit of my senses as well as your ladyship. I
295 have your own letter that induced me to the semblance I put
on; with the which I doubt not but to do myself much right,
or you much shame. Think of me as you please. I leave my
duty a little unthought of, and speak out of my injury.

The Madly-used Malvolio'

300 **Olivia**   Did he write this?

Feste   Ay, madam.

Duke   This savours not much of distraction.

Olivia   See him delivered, Fabian; bring him hither.

[*Exit* **Fabian**]

My lord, so please you, these things further thought on,
305 To think me as well a sister as a wife,
One day shall crown the alliance on't, so please you,
Here at my house and at my proper cost.

Duke   Madam, I am most apt to embrace your offer.
[*To* **Viola**] Your master quits you; and for your service done
310   him,
So much against the mettle of your sex,
So far beneath your soft and tender breeding,
And since you called me master for so long,
Here is my hand; you shall from this time be
Your master's mistress.

315 **Olivia**   A sister! You are she.

Feste   So I do, my lady. But to read *his* right mind is to read it like this. So pay attention, my princess, and lend me your ear . . .

Olivia   [*To* **Fabian**] You read it, fellow.

Fabian   [*taking the letter from* **Feste** *and reading it aloud*] '*By the lord, Madam: you do me wrong, and the world shall know of it. Though you have cast me into a dark room, and put me in the charge of your drunken cousin, I am as sane as your ladyship. I have your own letter which persuaded me to behave as I did, which will exonerate me and put you to shame. You can think what you like about me. I should be more polite, but I speak from a sense of grievance.*

The Madly-Used Malvolio'

Olivia   Did he write this?

Feste   Yes, madam.

Duke   This doesn't sound like madness.

Olivia   Set him free, Fabian, and bring him here.

[**Fabian** *goes*]

My lord, I hope you'll accept me as a sister-in-law rather than a wife when you've given more thought to the matter. If you agree, the ceremonies shall be on the same day, here at my house, and at my expense.

Duke   Madam, I accept your offer readily. [*To* **Viola**] Your master releases you: and because of your service to him – so unfeminine and so far beneath your gentle upbringing – and because you have called me 'master' for so long, here is my hand. [**Viola** *takes it*] Henceforth you are your master's wife.

Olivia   A sister, that's what you are!

[*Enter* **Fabian** *with* **Malvolio**]

Duke   Is this the madman?

Olivia   Ay, my lord, this same.
How now, Malvolio?

Malvolio   Madam, you have done me wrong,
Notorious wrong.

Olivia   Have I, Malvolio? No.

320 **Malvolio**   Lady, you have. Pray you peruse that letter.
You must not now deny it is your hand;
Write from it, if you can, in hand or phrase;
Or say 'tis not your seal nor your invention;
You can say none of this. Well, grant it then,
325   And tell me, in the modesty of honour,
Why you have given me such clear lights of favour
Bade me come smiling and cross-gartered to you,
To put on yellow stockings, and to frown
Upon Sir Toby and the lighter people;
330   And, acting this in an obedient hope,
Why have you suffered me to be imprisoned,
Kept in a dark house, visited by the priest,
And made the most notorious geck and gull
That e'er invention played on? Tell me why.

335 **Olivia**   Alas, Malvolio, this is not my writing,
Though, I confess, much like the character;
But, out of question, 'tis Maria's hand;
And now I do bethink me, it was she
First told me thou wast mad; then cam'st in smiling,
340   And in such forms which here were presupposed
Upon thee in the letter. Prithee, be content;
This practice hath most shrewdly passed upon thee;
But when we know the grounds and authors of it,
Thou shalt be both the plaintiff and the judge
Of thine own cause.

[**Fabian** *returns with* **Malvolio**]

Duke   Is this the madman?

Olivia   Yes, my lord, this is he. How are you, Malvolio?

Malvolio   Madam, you have wronged me. Wronged me
disgracefully.

Olivia   Have I, Malvolio? Surely not.

Malvolio   Lady, you have. Please read that letter. [*He hands*
Maria's *forgery to her*] You can't deny that you wrote it. Try
writing differently, if you can, in handwriting or style; or say
this isn't your seal; or that you didn't compose it. You can't
say any of this. Well, admit it and tell me, honestly, why you
gave me such favourable hints; asked me to come to you
smiling and cross-gartered; to put on yellow stockings; and
to frown at Sir Toby and the servants. And having done all
this with obedient expectation, why have you had me
imprisoned, kept in a dark place, visited by the parson, and
made the biggest fool and idiot that was ever tricked? Tell
me why?

Olivia   Alas, Malvolio, this isn't my handwriting, though I
admit it's very like it. Beyond a doubt it's Maria's. Now I
think about it, it was she who first told me you were mad.
Then you came in smiling, behaving as you were advised in
the letter. Be assured: this joke has been played on you very
cleverly, but when we know who perpetrated it and their
reasons, you shall be both judge and jury in your own case.

345 **Fabian**   Good madam, hear me speak,
     And let no quarrel nor no brawl to come
     Taint the condition of this present hour,
     Which I have wondered at. In hope it shall not,
     Most freely I confess, myself and Toby
350 Set this device against Malvolio here,
     Upon some stubborn and uncourteous parts
     We had conceived against him. Maria writ
     The letter at Sir Toby's great importance;
     In recompense whereof he hath married her.
355 How with a sportful malice it was followed,
     May rather pluck on laughter than revenge,
     If that the injuries be justly weighed
     That have on both sides passed.

     Olivia   Alas, poor fool, how have they baffled thee!

360 **Feste**   Why, 'some are born great, some achieve greatness, and
     some have greatness thrown upon them'. I was one, sir, in
     this interlude; one Sir Topas, sir; but that's all one. [*Imitating*
     Malvolio] 'By the Lord, fool, I am not mad.' But do you
     remember? 'Madam, why laugh you at such a barren rascal?
365 An you smile not, he's gagged'; and thus the whirligig of time
     brings in his revenges.

     Malvolio   I'll be revenged on the whole pack of you.

                                                            [*Exit*]

     Olivia   He hath been most notoriously abused.

     Duke   Pursue him, and entreat him to a peace.
370 He hath not told us of the captain yet;
     When that is known, and golden time convents,
     A solemn combination shall be made
     Of our dear souls. Meantime, sweet sister,
     We will not part from hence. Cesario, come;
375 For so you shall be, while you are a man;

Fabian   Dear madam, let me speak: may no dispute or future
brawl spoil the pleasure of this present time, which has
astonished me. In the hope that it won't, I freely confess
that Toby and I set this trap against Malvolio, because we
took exception to his haughty and discourteous manner.
Maria wrote the letter under instruction from Sir Toby; he
has married her in recompense. How the trick was followed
through with mischievous delight will no doubt cause more
laughter than desire for revenge, particularly if the
grievances on both sides are fairly weighed.

Olivia   [*to* **Malvolio**] Alas, you poor man, how they've made a
fool of you!

Feste   Why, 'some are born great, some achieve greatness,
and some have greatness thrust upon them'. I had a part in
this little play: I was Sir Topas, sir – but what of that?
[*Imitating* **Malvolio**] 'By the Lord, fool, I'm not mad.' But do
you remember? 'Madam, why do you laugh at such an
empty-headed rascal? If you don't laugh at him, he dries up.'
Such is how the wheel of fortune brings revenge!

Malvolio   I'll be revenged on the whole pack of you!

[*He goes*]

Olivia   He has been quite disgracefully wronged.

Duke   [*to* **Fabian**] Go after him and make your peace with him.
He hasn't told us about the Captain yet: when that's sorted
out, and the hour is right, we'll all be united in holy wedlock.
[*To* **Olivia**] Meantime, sweet sister, we'll stay here. Cesario,
for so I'll call you while you're dressed like a man, come: [*he*

But when in other habits you are seen,
Orsino's mistress, and his fancy's queen.

[*Exeunt all except* **Feste**]

Feste   [*Sings*]   *When that I was and a little tiny boy,*
                           With hey, ho, the wind and the rain;
380   *A foolish thing was but a toy,*
                           For the rain it raineth every day.

                           But when I came to man's estate,
                           With hey, ho, the wind and the rain;
                           'Gainst knaves and thieves men shut their gate,
385   *For the rain it raineth every day.*

                           But when I came, alas, to wive,
                           With hey, ho, the wind and the rain;
                           By swaggering could I never thrive,
                           For the rain it raineth every day.

390   *But when I came unto my beds,*
                           With hey, ho, the wind and the rain;
                           With toss-pots still had drunken heads,
                           For the rain it raineth every day.

                           A great while ago the world begun,
395   *With hey, ho, the wind and the rain;*
                           But that's all one, our play is done,
                           And we'll strive to please you every day.

[*Exit*]

offers her his arm] when you appear in other garments,
you'll be Orsino's wife, and queen of his love.

[*Everyone leaves but* **Feste**]

Feste   [*singing*]   *When that I was just a little tiny boy,*
            [*With hey, ho, the wind and the rain*]
            My foolishness was just a toy –
                For the rain it raineth every day.

            But when I came to man's estate
                [*With hey, ho, the wind and the rain*]
            'Gainst rogues and thieves men shut their
                  gate –
                For the rain it raineth every day.

            But when I came [*alas!*] *to wed*
                [*With hey, ho, the wind and the rain*]
            My boasting didn't keep us fed –
                For the rain it raineth every day.

            So when I came to go to bed
                [*With hey, ho, the wind and the rain*]
            With drunkards I would lay my head –
                For the rain it raineth every day.

            Long time ago, the world was begun
                [*With hey, ho, the wind and the rain*]
            But what of that? Our play is done –
                And we'll try to please you, every day.

[*He bows and leaves*]

Activities

Characters

Search the text to find answers to the following questions. They will help you to form personal opinions about the principal characters in the play. *Record any relevant quotations in Shakespeare's own words.*

Duke Orsino

1   From Orsino's first speech in *Act I Scene 1*, what evidence is there of

    a his taste for music

    b his sensitivity

    c his restlessness

    d his lovesickness?

    How do his final words in this scene suggest that he is in love with love?

2   **a** What does Valentine add to our understanding of Orsino at the beginning of *Act I Scene 4*?

    b How do we know from what the Duke himself says in the same scene

        i   that he is trusting in his confidences

        ii that he is persistent in his pursuit of Olivia

        iii that he is a student of courting techniques?

3   **a** In *Act II Scene 4* there is further evidence of Orsino's taste in music. From his remarks, what are his likes and dislikes?

    b There is also further evidence of his lovesickness. Which lines are most revealing?

c   What do we learn about
    i   his theories on age-relationships in marriage
    ii his theories about women's beauty
    iii his theories on the ability of women to experience
        love?

Do you think Shakespeare's sympathies were with Orsino, or
Viola, in their debate?

4   a   The Orsino of *Act V Scene 1* seems in a brighter mood at
        first than he has seemed before. Give examples of his good
        humour in the exchange with Feste.

    b   He also shows his authority in handling public business.
        Identify the speeches that best contrast with his private
        languor.

    c   Next, he confronts Olivia, having previously always com-
        municated with her through diplomatic messengers. How
        would you describe his moods
        i   when scorned by Olivia
        ii when shocked by the Priest's evidence concerning
            the marriage ceremony he has just conducted?

5   a   Look up the sea-captain's compliments about Orsino in
        Act I Scene 2 and Olivia's summary of his personal qualities
        in *Act I Scene 5*. How much of the praise seems to you to be
        well-earned?

    b   Which of these characteristics in particular makes his
        manner and actions at the end of the play credible and
        acceptable?

Viola

1   Viola's ability to adapt to circumstances is shown in the scene
    in which she first appears, *Act I Scene 2*.

    a   She asks brisk questions. How many?

    b   She quickly plans a course of personal action.

Activities

    i   What is her first inclination?
    ii What is her second, and why does she change?

2 In *Act 1 Scene 4*, three days later, Viola is in the Duke's employ
   and already 'no stranger'.

   a How do we know she quickly inspires confidence?
   b What do we learn of her personal appearance?

3 a Viola's first visit to Olivia on Orsino's behalf is in *Act I
      Scene 5*. Her arrival is announced
         i   by Maria
         ii by Sir Toby
         iii by Malvolio

      How does each describe her, and what further compliment
      to her is paid by Sir Toby in *Act III Scene 4*?

   b Olivia says Viola's approach seemed 'saucy', and that her
      address 'began rudely'.
         i   Give examples of Viola's pertness on her arrival.
         ii Do you think her manner is evidence of lack of self-
             confidence, or an ability to give as good as she gets, or
             both?

   c What evidence is there in the dialogue with Olivia that
         i   Viola is abrupt and straightforward
         ii dogged and determined
         iii proud
         iv not given to flattery?

   d What further insights into Viola's character come from
         i   What Olivia says about her
         ii the way Olivia reacts to the visit?

   e In the light of her performance as Orsino's messenger, how
      apt and accurate do you think is the description of her by
      her brother Sebastian in *Act II Scene I*?

4 Read *Act II Scene 4*.

   a How does Viola give expression to her secret love for
      Orsino without revealing it?

b Identify examples of her cryptic and ambiguous style of communication.

5 In *Act III Scene 1*, Viola

   a engages in good humoured banter with Feste. What does her soliloquy after his departure tell us about her astuteness?

   b engages in an exchange with Sir Toby. Who has the last word?

   c engages in an exchange of words with Olivia.

      i What part does double-meaning play in it?

      ii Which of Olivia's words vividly describe Viola's rejection of her advances?

      iii Which words of Olivia's in *Act III Scene 4* add further to our understanding of Viola's inflexible attitude and loyalty to Orsino?

6 Like Malvolio, Viola is a victim of Sir Toby's tricks. In *Act III Scene 4*

   a i What is the evidence to suggest that this is because she is a woman operating in a man's world?

      ii Which compliment of the Duke's at the end of the play is relevant to her behaviour in this episode?

   b What is the evidence to suggest that she fears the loss of her disguise more than the loss of her dignity?

7 In *Act V Scene 1*, Viola is under the greatest pressure from the consequences of mistaken identity.

   a Which lines show Viola at her most self-sacrificial in the cause of love?

   b Which line confirms that she puts duty to Orsino before her own self-defence?

   c With how many offences is Viola charged?

   d At what point does she choose to reveal herself, and what does this tell us of her priorities?

Olivia

1   Olivia does not appear in person in the play until *Act I Scene 5*, but we are well prepared in advance.

   a   What does Orsino say of her in *Act I Scene 1*?

   b   How is she described by the sea-captain in *Act I Scene 2*?

   c   What can we deduce about her character from the references to her made by Sir Toby and Maria in *Act I Scene 3*?

   d i   What aspect of her character is stressed in the discussion between Orsino and Viola in *Act I Scene 4*?

       ii   How does Olivia's reaction to the death of a brother apparently differ from that of Viola?

2   When we first meet her in *Act I Scene 5*, she first has a conversation with Feste, and then another with Malvolio.

   a   How does the former show that she has a sense of humour, even in grief?

   b   How does the latter show she is (i) tolerant;   (ii) well-balanced;   (iii) just?

3   **a**   Olivia is caring towards her family and servants.

       i   What example of this is to be found in *Act I Scene 5*?

       ii   What example is to be found in *Act III Scene 4*?

   b   She can be forceful with those who anger her.

       i   How does she do this through messages in *Act II Scene 3*?

       ii   How does she do this by personal intervention in *Act IV Scene 1*?

4   **a**   Olivia takes a firm line against the entreaties of Duke Orsino. How are her feelings evident from

       i   Valentine's report in *Act I Scene 1*?

       ii   her instructions to Malvolio in *Act I Scene 5*?

   b   She rejects Orsino (i) positively;   (ii) courteously. Which speech in *Act I Scene 5* illustrates this?

   c   She does so again on Viola's return visit in *Act III Scene 1*. Find examples which convey her feelings.

d She rejects Orsino in a face-to-face confrontation in *Act V Scene 1*.

    i Find four examples of her uncompromising attitude.

    ii Explain what has happened to make any other kind of response impossible.

5 For all that she has vowed to mourn her brother, and in spite of her apparent coldness, Olivia falls in love at first sight.

    a Look up Viola's description in *Act I Scene 5* of Orsino's love-sick adulation of her, and compare it with Viola's manner when acting as messenger. Explain how this latter may account for the speed with which Olivia catches 'the plague'.

    b How do Olivia's last lines in this scene indicate that she is now following her passions rather than her reason?

6 **a** In *Act III Scene 1*, Olivia openly reveals her love. Show from her first words how she does this with (i) dignity; (ii) modesty; (iii) restraint.

    b In the event, she cannot let Viola go without a further declaration of love. Show how once again she acknowledges the triumph of the heart over the head.

7 In *Act III Scene 4*, Olivia admits her infatuation.

    a How do her words to Viola show that she is intelligently self-aware and self-critical?

    b How do they also show that her obsession is an overriding one?

    c Do they account for 'this haste', and her marriage to Sebastian, as planned in *Act IV Scene 3*?

8 Olivia's last acts in the play are

    a to deal with Malvolio. How is the way she does this consistent with her kindness and consideration in the past?

    b to arrange the wedding ceremonies. How is her suggestion in accord with previous examples of generosity?

Activities

Malvolio

1   From his first words in *Act 1 Scene 5*, it is plain Malvolio takes an arrogant view of lesser mortals than himself.

    a   What does he think of Feste and his skill as a jester?

    b   What does he think of people who laugh at jesters' jokes?

    c   How does he distance himself even from his mistress, the Lady Olivia, in giving his opinion?

    d   How accurately does Olivia describe Malvolio's misguided attitude to life?

    e   What hint is there here that Malvolio is not universally respected?

2   In *Act II Scene 2*, Malvolio obeys instructions and gives Olivia's ring to Viola. How does he

    a   begin with a pompous rebuke

    b   deliver two cold messages

    c   treat Viola and the ring with haughty contempt?

3   In *Act II Scene 3*, Malvolio conveys Olivia's message to Sir Toby.

    a   Again he begins with a rebuke: a series of rhetorical questions. How do these express his disapproval of rowdy behaviour?

    b   Again he delivers a hard-hitting message. What does he say later to show that Olivia's disgust is also his own?

    c   Which line of Sir Toby's summarizes the case against men like Malvolio who expect others to behave as they do?

4   Maria is a fierce critic of Malvolio and the instigator of the practical joke against him which leads to his being 'notoriously abused'.

    a   Look up her catalogue of criticisms in *Act II Scene 3*. Which are the ones on which the plot against him is based?

    b   Critics, however, have credited Malvolio with some

virtues. Look up and consider

    i Fabian's reasons for disliking him [*Act II Scene 5*]. Who was in the right?

    ii Olivia's reference to qualities which she values, and her regard for his well-being, in *Act III Scene 4*.

Do you think Malvolio was 'only doing his job' as Steward by trying to maintain good order in a household that had recently suffered two bereavements?

5 There are three stages in the downfall of Malvolio:
    The setting of the trap [*Act II Scene 5*]
    The springing of the trap [*Act III Scene 4*]
    The humiliation [*Act IV Scene 2*]

a Find evidence in these scenes of
    i Malvolio's vanity with regard to women
    ii his ambition
    iii his pompousness
    iv his conceit
    v his absurdity.

b Decide whether there are grounds for sympathizing with Malvolio in his adversity by considering
    i Fabian's declared intention of making him 'mad indeed'.
    ii Sir Toby's declared intention of harassing him for 'pleasure'.
    iii Feste's unrelenting exploitation of the advantages he has over him.
    iv Malvolio's humility in adversity.
    v Malvolio's isolation and wretchedness.

c Trace the stages by which Malvolio persuades himself that Maria's hoax letter is a genuine one from Olivia.
    i What attracts his attention first?
    ii What phrase on the outside tempts him to proceed further?
    iii What is the next clue to the writer's identity?

    iv What are the clues written in rhyme?

    v What clues are there in the prose section?

d What further circumstantial evidence does Malvolio seize upon in *Act III Scene 4* to encourage his advances? Find three examples.

6 **a** Malvolio's rehabilitation begins in *Act V Scene 1* with Feste's delivery of the letter.

    i He first accuses Olivia. How does she react?

    ii Fabian then makes a confession. How does it differ from the facts as we know them?

    iii Sir Toby's gesture of 'recompense' is announced. Why might it have seemed more of a penance to an Elizabethan audience than a modern one?

    iv Feste reveals his part in the 'interlude'. Is his a case of 'he who laughs last laughs loudest', the privilege of a jester?

  b Malvolio leaves the play vowing revenge.

    i What privilege has Olivia earlier granted him in settling his 'own cause'?

    ii What case has Fabian put for 'laughter rather than revenge'?

    iii Do you think the Duke's appeal of 'a peace' will be successful?

Sir Toby Belch

1 As Maria points out in *Act I Scene 3*, Sir Toby does not confine himself 'within the modest limits of order.'

  a What is uncouth about the first sentence we hear him utter?

  b What do we learn about his life style?

  c What do we learn about his appearance?

  d What do we learn about his roguish ability to twist the truth?

    e   What do we learn about his sense of humour?

    f   What do we deduce about his relationship with Sir Andrew Aguecheek?

2 **a**   When he re-appears in *Act I Scene 5* he is 'half drunk'. Do you detect any occasions in the play when he is not?

    b   What two signs of inebriation does he show?

3 By his third appearance, there are many signs that he has progressed during the day to being fully drunk.

    a   What time of night is it?

    b   What is Sir Toby's way of saying that he likes a full tankard always at his elbow?

    c   What is significant about his choice of song?

    d   What evidence is there that Sir Toby becomes abusive when he is in his cups?

    e   Which of his words to Malvolio have been immortalized as a most telling retort to those who would moralize?

    f   Explain how the plot to humiliate Malvolio stems from Sir Toby's encounter with him in this scene.

4 In *Act II Scene 5* Malvolio falls for the bait while Sir Toby watches.

    a   What is amusing about Sir Toby's comments when in hiding?

    b   What does he say afterwards about Maria that turns out to be prophetic?

5 At the end of *Act III Scene 4* Sir Toby plans further humiliations for Malvolio.

    a   Whereas the first plot against him could be said to be revenge, what are Sir Toby's declared purposes in embarking on a second one?

    b   What reason does Sir Toby give in *Act IV Scene 2* for wishing to end the tormenting of his enemy?

6 a Sir Toby's abuse of his friendship with Sir Andrew is in evidence in *Act II Scene 3*. What signs are there that he is cheating his friend out of money?

b It is at its most marked in *Act III Scene 2*:
  i Why is Sir Toby's plan hardly that of a faithful friend?
  ii What does Sir Toby say to Fabian which confirms his lack of moral principle?

c It is seen in action in *Act III Scene 4*:
  i Explain how he makes his friend ridiculous; and
  ii how he turns the joke to profit.

d How does Sir Toby end the friendship in *Act V Scene 1*?

7 In *Act III Scene 4* and *Act IV Scene 1* Sir Toby is prepared to use his sword.

a Against whom does he first draw it, and why?

b Against whom does he draw it for the second time, and what mistake does he make?

c What is the final outcome of Sir Toby's aggressiveness, and how is it an example of 'the biter bit'?

Sir Andrew Aguecheek

1 a Maria introduces Sir Andrew to us in *Act I Scene 3*, when she refers to 'a foolish knight'. We learn subsequently
  i that he is rich. What is his reputed income?
  ii that he is a spendthrift. Who tells us this?
  iii that he is a quarreller. How is this later borne out in fact?
  iv that he is a coward. How is this later shown to be true?
  v that he has been set up as a rival to Orsino for the hand of Olivia. By whom and with what prospects?

b In the same scene, Sir Toby lists three of Sir Andrew's so-called accomplishments.

    i Shortly afterwards, Sir Andrew disproves one of them. Which is it, and what gives the game away?

    ii What skills does he claim to have?

    iii One of them is disproved in *Act III Scene 4*. Which is it?

c We also learn a little about his appearance.

    i How does Sir Toby describe his hair?

    ii How does Sir Andrew describe it, and what does this reveal of his character?

    iii What do we learn about his features at the end of *Act V Scene 1*?

d We discover he is easily led, and easily flattered. Find examples of each characteristic in *Act 1 Scene 3*, and in *Act III Scene 2*.

e Such is his weakness of character that he frequently echoes Sir Toby's phrases, or endorses his ideas.

    i Find examples in *Act I Scene 3; Act II Scene 3; Act III Scene 5*.

    ii Which of Viola's words in *Act III Scene 1* appeal to him so much that he resolves to memorize them for future use?

2 Sir Andrew's simplicity is shown in many ways.

a   i Foreign expressions baffle him. What are the examples in *Act I Scene 3* and *Act II Scene 2*?

    ii Some English words baffle him also. Find examples in *Act 1 Scene 3* and *Act II Scene 3*.

    iii Nonsense words give him child-like pleasure. Which appealed to him so much that he rewarded Feste with sixpence?

b He can be disarmingly frank about his own simplicity. Find examples in *Act II Scene 3* and *Act II Scene 5*.

c Sir Andrew's simplicity shows in his attitude to a challenge.

    i From what he says in *Act II Scene 3*, what is his naive

idea of a successful challenge?

ii Identify the reasons why his challenge to Viola [*Act III Scene 4*] is so 'excellently ignorant' that Sir Toby refuses to deliver it.

d 'I would rather than forty pounds I were at home', Sir Andrew says plaintively in *Act V Scene 1*, after Sebastian has beaten him.

i How has this situation come about?

ii What other evidence of his cowardice is there in *Act III Scene 4*?

Feste

1 Viola comments on the jester's art in a brief soliloquy in *Act III Scene 1*. Look up her speech and decide how far Feste matches up to the ideal.

2 **a** In *Act I Scene 5* Feste also has a brief soliloquy on the subject of his art. How does his last speech in the play fully vindicate what he says?

b What does he say to Olivia later in this scene – in Latin and English – which memorably makes the point that good fooling requires intelligence?

c Malvolio takes a different viewpoint. What is his assessment of Feste's skills?

d How does Olivia (i) criticize him; and (ii) come to his defence?

3 Feste's second appearance is at night with Sir Toby and Sir Andrew, in *Act II Scene 3*.

a Sir Andrew admires Feste, and pays him several compliments; he particularly admires his singing and his ability to speak learned nonsense.

i What examples are there in the play to confirm that he sings excellently and has a wide repertoire?

    ii Find other examples in this scene and in *Act IV Scene 2*, of his skill in what Sir Andrew calls 'very gracious fooling'.

4 In *Act II Scene 4*, Feste is at Duke Orsino's.

    a How do we know from what Curio says that he has been there before?

    b How does this provide the answer to the question put to him by Maria in *Act I Scene 5*?

    c Feste successfully begs money from the Duke. Find examples in *Act III Scene 1, Act IV Scene 1* and *Act V Scene 1* where he is equally successful in lining his pocket.

    d How shrewd is Feste's comment on Orsino's character?

5 **a** In *Act III Scene 1*, Feste says he is Olivia's 'corrupter of words'. Explain what he means, and find examples.

    b What else does he say later about 'foolery'! What is profound about his observation?

6 **a** In *Act IV Scene 2*, Feste is recruited by the conspirators to torment Malvolio in the guise of Sir Topas the curate. Sir Toby says of him 'The knave counterfeits well'. Find examples of his

      i vocal trickery; [In what circumstances does he demonstrate this skill again in *Act V Scene 1*?]

      ii learned nonsense.

    b At Sir Toby's suggestion, Feste again teases Malvolio: this time as himself. Which words of Malvolio's here would give Feste the sweetness of revenge he is seeking?

7 Feste ends the play with a song that has not always been as universally admired as it is today. Why do you think

    a The last word is given to the jester?

    b The song covers man's whole lifespan?

    c Reference is made to the world's great age?

    d The melancholy refrain is that 'the rain it raineth every day'?

    e The last two lines remind the listener that he has just watched a piece of theatrical entertainment?

Maria

1 At first, Maria is spokeswoman for her mistress; on the three occasions we first see her, she scolds her later allies.

In *Act 1 Scene 3* Sir Toby is reprimanded;

In *Act 1 Scene 5* Feste is rebuked;

In *Act II Scene 3* Sir Toby, Feste and Sir Andrew are jointly given a dressing down.

    a Explain each offence.

    b Give examples from each scene of Maria's good humour and wit.

    c Show from *Act II Scene 3* that

        i Maria dislikes Malvolio and

        ii is quick witted, ingenious, and a good organizer.

2 Once embarked on her practical joke, Maria shows several skills.

    a How does Malvolio confirm her skill as a forger by what he says in *Act II Scene 5*?

    b How is the letter so worded that it depends on Malvolio's own conceit and folly for its success?

    c What words of praise does she earn from her colleagues? List the complimentary epithets.

3 Maria stage-manages the humiliation of Malvolio from start to finish.

    a Is Fabian right to protect her in his speech of confession in *Act V Scene 1*?

    b Is marriage to Sir Toby a punishment or a reward?

Sebastian

1 Find evidence in *Act 1 Scene 2* and *Act II Scene 1* of
   a Sebastian's courage
   b his brotherly love
   c his gratitude as a friend.

2 How do we know from *Act III Scene 3* that he is
   a the sort of man who generates loyalty?
   b a cultured man?
   c a man to be trusted?

3 Several times in the play Sebastian makes quick decisions. Explain the circumstances in
   a *Act IV Scene 1*
   b *Act IV Scene 3.*

4 How do we know from *Act V Scene 1* what Sebastian looks like; how he speaks; how he dresses; and how he behaves?

Structure

There are two plots in *Twelfth Night*:

A   The story of Orsino, Olivia, Viola and Sebastian: the main plot.

B   The story of Sir Toby Belch, Sir Andrew Aguecheek and their humiliation of Malvolio: the sub-plot.

1   By *Act II Scene 1*, all the characters have been introduced.

    a   Which two characters in Story B are directly linked to Story A, and how?

    b   In Story A
       i   How is Olivia linked to Orsino?
       ii   How is Viola linked to Orsino?
       iii   How do Olivia and Viola come to be linked?
       iv   How does the brother-sister relationship linking Viola and Sebastian cause complications involving the characters of Story B?

    c   In Story B,
       i   How is Malvolio linked to Olivia in the main plot and Sir Toby in the sub-plot?
       ii   How is Sir Andrew Aguecheek linked to Olivia in the main plot?
       iii   How do Sir Toby and Sir Andrew come to be linked to Viola in the main plot?
       iv   What incident brings them most closely together, and what is the reason for the comic complications?

2   Interwoven into the two plots is the character of Feste the jester.

    a   What evidence is there that he sometimes resides at Duke Orsino's house, though he is part of Olivia's household?

    b   How is he involved in Story A and Story B?

Themes

The opening lines of the play are about love, and so is the play as a whole.

1   Duke Orsino is in love with love. Find as many examples as you can of his love-sick utterances
      i   about love itself
     ii   about his love for Olivia in particular.

2   Olivia experiences love at first sight.
      i   Look up what she says about how 'one may catch the plague' [*Act I Scene 5*].
     ii   Trace the scene in which she argues that 'love sought is good, but given unsought is better.'

3   Viola suffers from secret love.
      i   In which scene does she first reveal it to the audience?
     ii   In which subsequent scene does she come closest to revealing it to Orsino?

4   Malvolio is a victim of self-love.
      i   Look up Olivia's shrewd criticism in *Act I Scene 5*. How does it compare with Maria's on the same subject in *Act II Scene 3*?
     ii   Select examples of his conduct and speech to illustrate the high opinion he has of himself.

Close reading

Read the original Shakespeare and [if necessary] the modern transcription, to gain an understanding of the speeches and extracts below. Then concentrate entirely on the original in answering the questions.

1   *If music be the food of love, play on* [*Act I Scene 1*]

   a   What does Orsino hope that music can do for him?

   b   What does he particularly like about the piece the musicians are playing?

   c   The simile which begins in the fifth line compares musical notes with the sound of the wind:

      i   how does the verb 'breathes' enhance the imagery?

     ii   Look up the comments of Sir Toby on Feste's singing in *Act II Scene 3*. How do they help to explain the association here of sound with fragrance?

   d   Orsino stops the musicians. What, in fact, has been the effect of the surfeit that he requested?

   e   In his apostrophe to the spirit of love, the Duke makes a comparison with the sea.

      i   How does this image give scale to his point about love's 'capacity'?

     ii   How does the conclusion he reaches add to his melancholy?

2   *Make me a willow cabin at your gate* [*Act I Scene 5*]

   a   To what question is this an answer?

   b   Why is the willow an appropriate tree to associate with grief?

   c   The object of Viola's strategy as described here is to generate pity. Which phrases seem to you designed to wring the heart?

    d Explain why the echoes from the hills are described as 'babbling gossip'.

3 *There is no woman's sides* [*Act II Scene 4*]

    a The Duke begins by giving three reasons why women cannot match him in his suffering: list them.

    b He then likens love to the business of eating.

        i Explain his distinction between the liver and the palate.

        ii Explain his simile of the sea, and relate it to a similar point in his first speech in the play.

    c **i** How would you describe the tone of the Duke's references to women?

        ii Is there one word in particular which epitomizes it?

4 *A blank, my lord. She never told her love* [*Act II Scene 4*]

    a What was 'a blank'?

    b Explain how the simile in the second line helps to explain why the subject of the speech went pale.

    c How do the two colours mentioned relate to sickness?

    d A memorable simile precedes the question 'Was not this love indeed?' Explain why it is so effective in conveying the idea of suppressed grief.

    e What is ironical about the phrase 'we men'?

    f Which words in the last line are balanced against each other?

    g About whom is Viola really speaking?

5 *This fellow's wise enough to play the fool* [*Act III Scene 1*]

    a Explain the paradox in the first line.

    b Which three factors must a wise fool take into consideration to be a success?

    c How does the hawking simile illustrate a temptation that he must resist?

    d Why are the last two lines in rhyme?

Activities

6 *Oh! what a deal of scorn looks beautiful* [*Act III Scene 1*]

    a The first two lines contain ideas which seem to be contradictory.

    b Explain the effectiveness of the contrast in conveying the speaker's mixed feelings.

    c Two comparisons explain why love cannot be concealed. How does each add to an understanding of love's irrepressible qualities?

    d What does Olivia say conflicts with her passion, but unsuccessfully?

    e Rhyme is a feature of this speech. Which couplet is given a special emphasis by means of it?

7 *Oh ho! do you come near me now* [*Act III Scene4*]

    a This prose passage is a soliloquy, in which Malvolio reveals the workings of his mind. How does it show from the beginning that he is determined to twist facts to suit himself?

    b Does Malvolio accurately convey the contents of the hoax letter, or does he elaborate upon them?

    c Explain how 'fellow' might have a different meaning to Malvolio from the one which Olivia intended.

    d How is Malvolio's ecstasy conveyed in the language he uses to convince himself he is right?

    e How do his last remarks show his self-righteousness?

8 *This is the air; that is the glorious sun* [*Act IV Scene 3*]

    a What is Sebastian debating to himself in this soliloquy?

    b Why does he begin by referring to the air, the sun, and a pearl?

    c How might Antonio help him in his perplexity?

    d Why does he conclude that 'There's something in it that's deceivable'?

9 *Why should I not, had I the heart to do it* [*Act V Scene 1*]

    a The Duke hints at an act of desperation; which phrase at the beginning of his speech makes us realize that Viola is not in real danger?

    b In his passion, the Duke moves from jealous suspicion to jealous certainty in four lines. Identify the relevant words.

    c Animal and bird imagery is the vehicle for Orsino's direct threats. Explain how they convey his profound feelings.

10 *When that I was and a little tiny boy* [*Act V Scene 1*]

    a What stages in the life of man are featured in Feste's song?

    b   i Each verse mentions a human weakness or folly. Identify them.

        ii Are these examples of misbehaviour applicable only to [say] the Elizabethan age, or are they of all time?

    c Each verse has the same refrain. Can you think of an explanation why Feste's song repeatedly mentions 'the wind and the rain', and tells us four times that 'the rain it raineth every day' when he could, if he wished, celebrate warmth and sunshine?

    d The last verse begins by referring to mankind's lengthy history as though Feste intends to make a philosphic point.

        i What does he do instead?

        ii What do you think might have been Shakespeare's purpose in ending the play on this note?

Examination questions

The following are typical of the kind of examination questions set by the major examining boards:

1   *Twelfth Night* is a comedy, the subject of which is love'. How does love affect the characters in the play in different ways?

2   Choose any *one* character in the play and say why, and by what means, he or she is made an object of ridicule. How far do you sympathize with the character of your choice?

3   Give a detailed account of Malvolio's discovery of the letter and of his appearance before Olivia dressed in yellow stockings. What do the two scenes reveal of his character?

4   Is Malvolio a character with whom you can have sympathy, or did he deserve his fate?

5   'Twelfth Night is a play about deceit; as the play progresses, people learn the truth about themselves.' Do you agree?

6   Explain the complications which arise from Viola's decision to disguise herself as a page, and say how she deals with the problems.

7   What would be the loss to *Twelfth Night* if the Sir Toby/Sir Andrew scenes were cut?

8   At the end of the play, Feste sings his strange song. What, if any, is the point of it?

9   Give an account of Orsino's wooing of Olivia through Viola, and say what you learn from it of the characters of all three.

10   'He hath been most notoriously abused'. Give a detailed account of the part played by Malvolio in *Twelfth Night*.

11   Compare and contrast the characters of Viola and Olivia.

12   What complications ensue from the appearance of Sebastian in Illyria?

13 What part does music and song play in *Twelfth Night*?

14 'This fellow's wise enough to play the fool'. Explain Viola's comment on Feste's skills, and give some examples of his jesting in action.

15 Give an account of Sir Andrew's challenge to Viola and the subsequent duel, explaining (a) how the episode contributes to our understanding of their characters and (b) how it enhances the comic element in the play.

16 'Sir Toby Belch is a drunkard and a rogue, yet he has endearing qualities which make him popular with audiences'. How far do you agree?

17 Say what you know of Duke Orsino's attitude (a) to love; (b) to marriage and (c) to women.

18 What part does *either* Maria *or* Feste play in the action of *Twelfth Night*?

19 'In *Twelfth Night*, humour arises (a) from action and situation and (b) from characters and words'. Give illustrations of each, and say which has given you most enjoyment.

20 Describe Viola's first interview with Olivia in *Act I*, and contrast it with her return visit in *Act III*, when Olivia reveals her love. To what extent has Viola developed through experience?

One-word-answer quiz

1 Who did Olivia say was 'sick of self love'?

2 By what name was Sebastian first known to Antonio?

3 By what name was Viola first known to Duke Orsino?

4 Who claimed he was 'dog at a catch'?

5 What was the signature at the end of the letter found by Malvolio?

6 Who was 'wise enough to play the fool'?

7 What, according to Viola, was 'not a grise'?

8 What did Duke Orsino think music might be?

9 What was the name of the priest whom Feste impersonated when visiting Malvolio?

10 What present did Olivia give to Sebastian?

11 What present did she give to Viola?

12 At what was a certain daughter smiling?

13 What, according to Feste, 'does walk about the orb like the sun'?

14 How many times did Orsino give Feste money when he begged for it?

15 For how many years did Olivia vow to mourn her dead brother?

16 For how many months did Antonio shelter Sebastian?

17 In which town in England was there a bed requiring an exceptionally large sheet?

18 What was the name of Duke Orsino's ship, captured by Antonio?

19 What was the name of the father of Sebastian and Viola?

20 What was his home town?

21 What was the name of the surgeon Sir Toby hoped would attend to his wounds?

22 Which lady was said by Malvolio to have 'married the yeoman of the wardrobe'?

23 Who 'at the point of death' was said to have killed what he loved?

24 Who was all the daughters of her father's house, and all the brothers too?

25 Whose face was 'excellently done, if God did all'?

26 Who was 'adored once, too'?

27 What, according to Viola, was 'a wickedness wherein the pregnant enemy does much'?

28 What, according to Feste, is 'a stuff will not endure'?

29 What was the colour which, according to Maria, the lady Olivia abhorred?

30 What did Viola's father have upon his brow?

31 With what material did Sir Toby tell Malvolio to clean his chain?

32 At which inn did Antonio book rooms?

33 What was the name of Duke Orsino's nephew?

34 Aboard which ship did he lose his leg?

35 How much did Sir Andrew give Feste for his 'leman'?

36 How much did Sir Toby give Feste for a song?

37 How much did Sir Andrew give him too?

38 What, according to Malvolio, 'does make some obstruction in the blood'?

39 Who was said to have 'a most weak pia-mater'?

40 What kind of a cabin did Viola say she would build at Olivia's gate?

41 Whose father had a daughter who 'sat like Patience on a monument'?

42 Whose picture was on Olivia's personal seal?

43 How old was Viola when her father died?

44   What was the name of Sir Andrew's grey horse?

45   What kind of song did Sir Toby ask Feste to sing?

46   What do some 'have thrust upon them' according to the letter found by Malvolio?

47   What kind of handwriting did Olivia use?

48   What word did Feste say was overworn?

49   What word did he use instead?

50   Who, according to Orsino, 'are as roses, whose fair flower being once displayed, doth fall that very hour'?

What's missing?

1   Did you never see a picture of . . .?
2   Be not afraid of greatness; . . .
3   I marvel your ladyship takes delight in such a barren rascal . . .
4   Come, sir, you peevishly threw it to her; and her will is . . .
5   Mark it, Cesario; it is old and plain; The spinsters and . . .
6   For such as I am, all true lovers are . . .
7   I see you what you are; you are too proud; But . . .
8   Enough! no more . . .
9   If it be aught to the old tune, my lord, It is . . .
10 This is to give a dog and . . .
11 Lady, you are the cruellest she alive, It . . .
12 What says Quinapulus? '. . .'
13 Were you a woman, as the rest goes even, I should . . .
14 What a plague means my niece to . . .?
15 Make me a willow cabin at your gate, And . . .
16 That face of his I do remember well; Yet . . .
17 What is love? 'Tis not hereafter; . . .
18 Oh, he's drunk, Sir Toby, an hour agone; . . .
19 Oh, it came o'er my ear like the sweet sound That . . .
20 Thou shalt hold the opinion of Pythagorus ere . . .
21 Away before me to sweet beds of flowers . . .
22 I am a great eater of beef, and I believe . . .
23 So please my lord, I might not be admitted, But from her handmaid do return this answer: . . .
24 Dost thou think, because thou art virtuous, there . . .?
25 One face, one voice, one habit, and two persons . . .

26 How easy is it for the proper-false . . .

27 When that I was and a little tiny boy . . .

28 For women are as roses . . .

29 This is the air; that is the glorious sun . . .

30 If music be the food of love . . .

31 If thou entertainest my love, let it appear in . . .

32 I hate ingratitude more in a man Than . . .

33 Let still the woman take An elder than herself, so . . .

34 If one should be a prey, how much the better To . . .

35 Oh, you are sick of self-love, Malvolio, and . . .

36 *My* servant, sir? 'Twas never merry world Since . . .

37 Love sought is good, but . . .

38 In sooth, thou wast in very gracious fooling last night, when thou spokest of . . .

39 Oh time, thou must untangle this, not I . . .

40 I am no fee'd post, lady; keep your purse; . . .

41 I did impeticos thy gratillity, for . . .

42 This is a practice As full of labour as a wise man's art . . .

43 'Tis beauty truly blent, whose red and white . . .

44 He is very well-favoured, and he speaks very shrewishly; one would think . . .

45 Many a good hanging prevents . . .

46 Go, hang yourselves all! You are . . .

47 Disguise, I see thou art a wickedness Wherein . . .

48 In nature there's no blemish but the mind; . . .

49 Oh what a deal of scorn looks beautiful . . .

50 She pined in thought, And with a green and yellow melancholy . . .